THE MASTER ARCHITECT SERIES

J. J. Pan and Partners

潘 冀 聯 合 建 築 師 事 務 所

THE MASTER ARCHITECT SERIES

J. J. Pan and Partners

潘 冀 聯 合 建 築 師 事 務 所

images
Publishing

Published in Australia in 2012 by
The Images Publishing Group Pty Ltd
ABN 89 059 734 431
6 Bastow Place, Mulgrave, Victoria 3170, Australia
Tel: +61 3 9561 5544 Fax: +61 3 9561 4860
books@imagespublishing.com
www.imagespublishing.com

National Library of Australia Cataloguing-in-Publication entry:

Author: Pan, Joshua Jih, 1942-
Title: J. J. Pan and Partners / Joshua J. Pan.
ISBN: 978 186470 430 3 (hbk.)
ISBN: 978 186470 469 3 (pbk.)
Series: Master architect series.
Subjects: J J Pan and Partners—History.
                 Architects—Taiwan.
                 Architecture, Modern—20th century—Taiwan.
                 Architecture—Taiwan.
Dewey Number: 720.951249

Edited by Mark Cleary and Debbie Ball

Designed by The Graphic Image Studio Pty Ltd, Mulgrave, Australia
www.tgis.com.au

Pre-publishing services by United Graphic Pte Ltd, Singapore
Printed on 150 gsm Quatro Silk Matt paper

IMAGES has included on its website a page for special notices in relation to this
and our other publications. Please visit www.imagespublishing.com.

Contents

A Critical and Innovative Engagement

In celebration of the 30th anniversary of founding J. J. Pan and Partners

J. J. Pan and Partners is held in high esteem in Taiwan for mastering a holistic way of architectural practice, guided by Professor Joshua J. Pan's belief that "A successful piece of architecture should be a project that is innovative in design, satisfies the client and is executed flawlessly." Naturally, achieving a balanced excellence in the process of design, service and delivery has become the hallmark of the firm.

The firm has evolved and progressed along with the comprehensive development pattern in Taiwan—such as, the urban and institutional expansions, the societal accumulation of wealth, and the strategic shift of economic strength from low-tech to high-tech industries. The work done by the firm thus encompasses a broad range of building types, and demonstrates a concentrated effort in enlivening and enriching the environment and people's lives.

Looking ahead, the firm's future is sustained by a team imbued with fresh vitality through a well arranged succession process. The teamwork exhibited has proven to be a multivalent mode of competitiveness with a keen design capacity.

Building the Innovative Milieu

The most widespread influence of J. J. Pan and Partners should be its active involvement in formulating the architecture of 'innovative milieu' in Taiwan. This innovative milieu has been based on the government supported: science and technology parks, campuses and schools, R & D facilities, hotels, libraries, congregating spaces, and transportation infrastructure. Together these nodes form a new life/work/communication prosperity sphere driven by innovative technologies and services. The agglomeration of these facilities has gradually formed an innovative corridor along the western half of the Island, and constitutes the bulk of J. J. Pan and Partners' commissioned projects. The high-tech I.T. industry especially has become a niche building type for the firm.

2

3

1

This high-tech architecture requires highly precise design and delivery in order to achieve the required vibration resistance, absolute cleanness and a fast track schedule. The disciplined performance of the firm's operation and its restrained design approach, matches well with the stringent and pragmatic demands of this thriving industry. However, J. J. Pan and Partners still manages to further its design elaboration in shaping a friendly environment and presenting a humane appearance for every project it is responsible for.

Projects such as the Lien Hwa Headquarters (Fig.1 & pp.90-99), MediaTek Headquarters (pp.78-89), and Winbond Technology Building (Fig.3), are among the most brilliant I.T. buildings created through the mature composition of formal interplay. Roofs, terraces, atriums, sunken plazas or gardens, linked by corridors, bridges, arcades, are organized in distinct and deliberate fashion. Several other projects, such as the Holistic Education Village at Chung Yuan Christian University (Fig.2), Fleur de Chine Hotel (Fig.4 & pp.124-133), and National Taichung Digital Library (pp.220-225) are also remarkable works along the innovative milieu corridor. The firm has even extended its expertise to Mainland China, as demonstrated by the extraordinary examples of Kingland Mansion in Shanghai (Fig.5), and ZyXEL R & D Campus in Wuxi (Fig.6 & pp.34-41).

The effort by the firm and its progressive clients over the past decades has created an innovative landscape par excellence. To some extent, this is a contribution of the "Made in Taiwan" economic phenomenon; which demonstrates not only value-added economic thinking, but also an intention to upgrade the physical, and cultural environment.

Compositional Form Defining the New

From early on, the firm has developed a distinctive formal strategy of elaborating the compositional dualism of mass/void, solid/transparent, figure/ground, vertical /horizontal, square/round … and so on, to bring forth a sense of urbanity to a project and its context. This strategy specifically scales down the monolithic volume of the production space that I.T. fabrication typically demands. In the skillful hands of J. J. Pan and Partners, complex functions and forms are woven together in plans and sections to compose a vivid image of humanist touches.

4

5

6

The compositional strategy is equally applicable to commissions for rebuilding or expanding existing school campuses, which require reintegrating the existing site relationships to the new constructions. The most successful projects of this type, reformulate a surprisingly new wholeness by introducing a structural change into the existing surroundings.

Among these well executed works, the Founder's Memorial Library at Chinese Culture University (Fig.7), is an elaborate horizontal and vertical composition, in accordance with the existing building in front of it, the post-disaster reconstruction project for Nan Kai College (Fig.8), totally changes the original character of the campus with a new layout pattern, and the new buildings for Ginling Girls' High School (pp.178-183) provide an eye-catching figure/void composition.

In sum, the compositional strategy applied by J. J. Pan and Partners is mostly asymmetrical, subtly laid out, letting the void space flow fluidly, or subverting the existing axial profile. The consequence usually reveals an assertive insight into the new, yet unknown wholeness, and liberates the status quo from the site.

Responsive Skin-Layering

If the Library for Chung Yuan Christian University (Fig.9), is regarded as the first milestone work of the firm employing a figurative tripartite composition of top, body and base, then the Da-Sha House at Chinese Culture University (Fig.10), is the watershed of applying a screen layer on the façade of the existing building, to integrate the new addition—a smart skin responsive to the media-active urban environment of downtown Taipei.

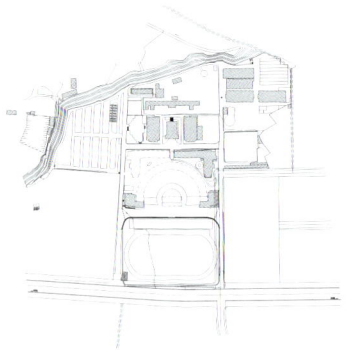

7

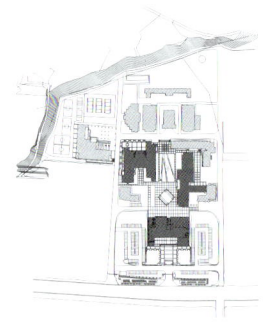

Campus plan after the earthquake   New campus plan

8

9

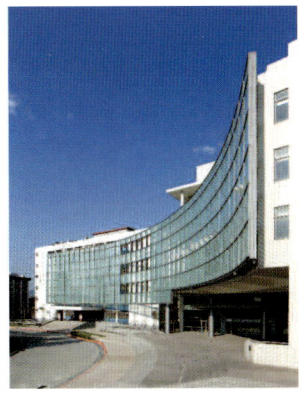

10   11

12

Neo Solar Power Office Building Complex (Fig.13 & pp.134-139) is composed of trapezoid glass panels that compensates the mundane trunk of production space on the back side. In both cases, the dramatic-light skins of the buildings, work as communicative layers, conveying the innovative image for the high-tech enterprises.

The application of layering skin is technically similar to a curtain wall, but differs from the mute curtain wall that typically only tightly wraps around a box-shaped building. As in all the cases mentioned above, the skin layering reveals or performs. It either conveys something different than the body behind it, or performs an unexpected play. It is an extra layer of cultural element as well.

A similar example is the continuous and translucent-curved glass screen for the Research Building for College of Medicine, Fu Jen Catholic University (Fig.11 & pp.172-177), which deliberately unites the new and existing buildings, and introduces an encompassed sense of closure that is a much better fit to the existing circular auditorium.

Other examples include the fluctuating glass curves applied to the façade of Quanta Display TFT/LCD Plant (Fig.12 & pp. 202-205) that deftly softens the huge volume of fabricated space behind. The irregularly folding northern façade of the

13

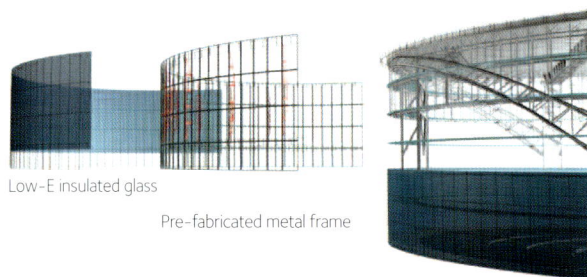

Low-E insulated glass

Pre-fabricated metal frame

Steel cantilevered arch with unbounded brace frame

14

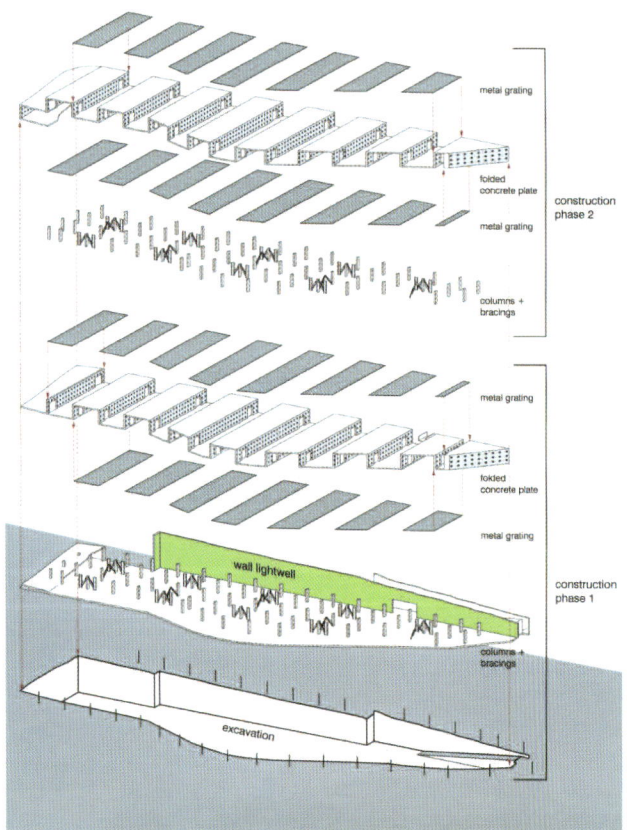

metal grating

folded
concrete plate

construction
phase 2

metal grating

columns +
bracings

metal grating

folded
concrete plate

metal grating

wall lightwell

construction
phase 1

columns +
bracings

excavation

15

Structure-Form and Monadic Envelope

The Gymnasium of Chinese Culture University (Fig.14 & pp. 110-117) can be seen as another milestone for the firm's very recent works. Analogous to the I.T. complex of a large manufacturing plant with a small office function, it houses both sport and classroom uses; with the latter configured as wings, to comply with the surrounding campus, and the former as a voluminous ellipsoidal body to compliment the curved contour of the mountains. The project is a bold mixture of tectonic and expressionist approaches, and shows aggression and compliance at the same time. It is from this project that two design trends of the firm emerge.

One is the structure-form, masterly represented by the Scooter Garage for National Chiao Tung University (Fig.15). Its folding concrete slabs work as both structural support and finished form, while ingeniously satisfying the parking function. For the Stockholm Library Competition Project (pp.194-197), double-helix configured ramps interweave around an open funnel-like light well, serving as an intriguing antithesis to the adjacent library designed by G. Asplund, which is well known for its spectacular round atrium inside. In the case of Flagship Building for Huashan Cultural Creative Center (pp.212-219), interlocked column-free floors and trussed floors, exhibit a straight-forward expression of form and structure.

The other trend goes toward the monadic envelope. The Church of Suang-Lien Center for the Elderly (pp.154-163), Taoyuan International Airport Access MRT Station (pp.164-171), HTC R & D Project (pp.198-201), and National Taichung Digital Library (Fig.16 & pp.220-225) are remarkable projects of this category. They demonstrate completed landmarks or public nodes with a singular form and cutting

16

edge material. Not just an up-to-date digital style follower, the firm implies with this approach a transcendence from the functional problem-solving to the imageneering maneuver, addressing the new civic and public concern.

Coinciding with Taiwan's progression to a "developed-nation" status, both the tectonic and the expressionist practices seem to provide a new societal imagination for the general public. This mission is surely appropriate for the firm, that is always committed itself to mastering the fundamentals yet dares to be radical when the right opportunities arise.

Design-Oriented with Critical Capacity

With its sustaining endeavor, J. J. Pan and Partners have already developed a very convincing design discourse over the past thirty years. Employing Habermas' concept, the firm's main contribution is having helped to formulate the very shift of the world ruled by instrumental rationality to the one by communicative concern during the period of rapid development in Taiwan. The formal strategies it has applied to the various kinds of projects speak of a discourse centered on "culture". To make the high-tech fabrication shed more friendly, to communicate with the public by attached layers and to explore the tectonic and expressionist possibilities for a new civic vision, all contribute to developing a critical sense of contemporary culture.

The critical strength revealed in all of J. J. Pan's works comes from a keen apprehension to strive for a new wholeness unseen before the firm's intervention. This strength is logical and robust because the practice is fundamentally based on a holistic view of architecture as a social and cultural engagement. For J. J. Pan and Partners, a combination of the Christian spirit of providence and the "Confucian" pursuit for ultimate goodness indeed guarantees a commitment to critical and innovative architecture.

Shih-wei Lo, Ph.D.
Architect
Professor, Department of Architecture, Tunghai University

What I have learned witnessing the evolution of J. J. Pan and Partners

I had trouble finding J. J. Pan and Partners' office during my first visit in 1998. Located at the end of an alleyway in a residential neighborhood behind Ren-Ai Road, it contained a maze-like organic seating arrangement, a cozy family working environment, and a company cafeteria within to allow employees to eat as if in their dining room at home, defying any pre-conceptions I had about Taiwan's largest architectural firm.

Mr. Pan walked in after working hours to check on the progress of a competition project, while I was chatting with two of the project architects. I saw Mr. Pan's red marks on the transmittals to be sent to clients and his red lines in the drawings ready for another revision on the table; I heard his design comments on the site plan and the critiques of the spatial arrangements for the buildings, and I was asked to offer my opinion on the design concept for the project. Sincere, humble, authoritative, demanding, self-critical, determined yet very passionate about design was my first impression of Mr. Pan.

Though I have never worked with J. J. Pan and Partners, I have remained a close friend of the firm's—a design critic observing what they do, a lecturer whose students see the firm as an employer of choice, and a design professional drawing inspiration from their work. J. J. Pan and Partners not only knows how to deliver projects with design excellence and high technical competence, understands operational efficiency and how to maintain sustainable and profitable growth, but the firm also has an organizational agility and engages with its employees. In addition to these attributes necessary for a successful design practice, Mr. Pan welcomes critical comments, encourages dynamic design discussions; stands up to regulatory authorities whose decisions contradict professional advice; continues to improve his knowledge and experience, by attending professional lectures and symposiums; and contributes both professionally and personally to the greater society.

Mr. Pan is a strong leader who leads by doing, influences by being present, implements by taking care of the fundamentals, succeeds by working hard, and advances by believing there is no limit to improvement. There is an extremely low turnover rate at J. J. Pan and Partners because Mr. Pan believes people are the firm's true asset, and the knowledge his staff has accumulated over the years is the foundation of the practice. Investing in people, cultivating the growth of individuals, providing a platform for the continued development of career paths, and growing with its people are critical to the success of the firm. Mr. Pan's beliefs are reflected in the spirit and culture of the firm, as people are inspired to follow his lead. Growth is not seen as a target, but an inevitable result of things being done right.

As a young professional entering the world of architectural practice in Taiwan in the late 90s, despite my inexperience and perhaps my naivety, the critical opinions I offered during my casual visits to the J. J. Pan and Partners' office, were always taken seriously by Mr. Pan. When valid, they became an integral part of the projects. Mr. Pan told me there is no seniority in creativity and professionalism. If a point is well made and is right, why hesitate to adopt it, only because it challenged the authority—him?

Over the past decade, it is evident from the significant diversification in the range of projects undertaken and the number of design competitions participated in that J. J. Pan and Partners has evolved. Beginning by simply focusing on satisfying client needs and ensuring quality standards and functional requirements were met in the projects it worked on, the firm now provides integrated design services that address structural innovation; optimum cost and construction program management; and urban, landscape and interior design solutions. The firm now also places strong emphasis on conceptual design that draws inspiration from technical advancements, sustainability, cultural value and heritage, and architectonic aesthetics to enrich design and place making.

J. J. Pan and Partners builds on its strength by undertaking institutional work such as library and academic buildings. Façade renovations and building additions to the existing Da-Sha House at the Chinese Culture University (Fig.1), a parking structure for scooters at the Chiao-Tung University (Fig.2), and the Taipei bus shelter prototype (pp.48–51), clearly demonstrate how great projects don't need to be on a grand and massive scale. Great projects are great because site constraints were turned into opportunities, budget limitations prompted design innovation, and construction challenges inspired creative delivery methodologies.

Enhancing Taiwan's unique I.T. building typology by not simply treating each as a mega-fabricating plant, but taking every opportunity to convince the client to invest more and take on social responsibilities in integrating the building mass with the surrounding context and to improve the built environment through sustainable green building design have been constant goals for J. J. Pan and Partners, and the firm has put a lot of effort into achieving them. To Mr. Pan, these are professional obligations and responsibilities rather than accomplishments.

Being a witness and outsider participating in J. J. Pan and Partners' transformation and evolution over the past years has truly been an ongoing learning process. What I have observed in the internal and external workings of the firm, is that which is essential to the development of a unique architectural design practice. It has been inspiring for me, as an architect: to see professional ethics upheld, operational models transformed, design quality assured, creativity embraced, design concepts implemented and, most importantly, people inspired, and integrity advocated. As J. J. Pan and Partners enters its fourth decade and expands its operational bases to different geographies, how will the firm's core values and vision see it evolve next? Although I cannot predict where J. J. Pan and Partners will be in the next decade, I sincerely hope it continues to grow, evolve and enhance our "built" environment.

Nancy Lin, AIA
Regional Director,
Planning, Design + Development, Hong Kong
AECOM

艸丮吉 —Sustainability, Professionalism and Discourse

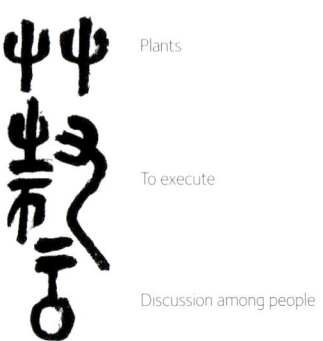

Plants

To execute

Discussion among people

Achieving a balance between excellent design, meticulous execution, and efficient delivery in a holistic architectural practice has always been a challenge for architects. Since the founding of J. J. Pan and Partners in 1981, it has been evident that our strong focus on mastering design, service & delivery has become the firm's hallmark.

The firm's approach to these three distinct aspects of architecture can be best understood through the Chinese character 丮 (etymology of 藝yì, art). A philological analysis of the character reveals three distinct parts: The top portion is a pictogram representing "plants"; the middle portion indicates "to execute", and the bottom portion implies "discussion". "Yì" best summaries J. J. Pan and Partners' core values, as these elements translate to "sustainability", "professionalism" and "discourse" – three essential components of art, which we diligently pursue in architecture through all of our projects.

At J. J. Pan and Partners, the healthy discourse between the architecture and the past, present and future, provides the context and serves as the fountainhead of all designs. The firm draws upon its innate critical understanding of regionalism to create designs immersed in their sense of

place, while at the same time contributing to the progression of "international" architecture that transcends its local context. The firm honors history by incorporating vernacular culture early in the design process, as these principles are perfected through time and instill the essential human touch into architecture.

For example, the Pegatron Shanghai Campus (Fig.1 & pp. 100-109) upholds local culture and wisdom by conceptualizing the South Anhui Province vernacular "Hui" architectural style. Its courtyard parti portrays the "working rice paddy" imagery, a metaphor resembling the "integration of literary and labor", emulating the collective spirit of R & D

1

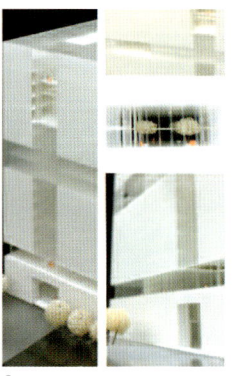

2　　　　　3

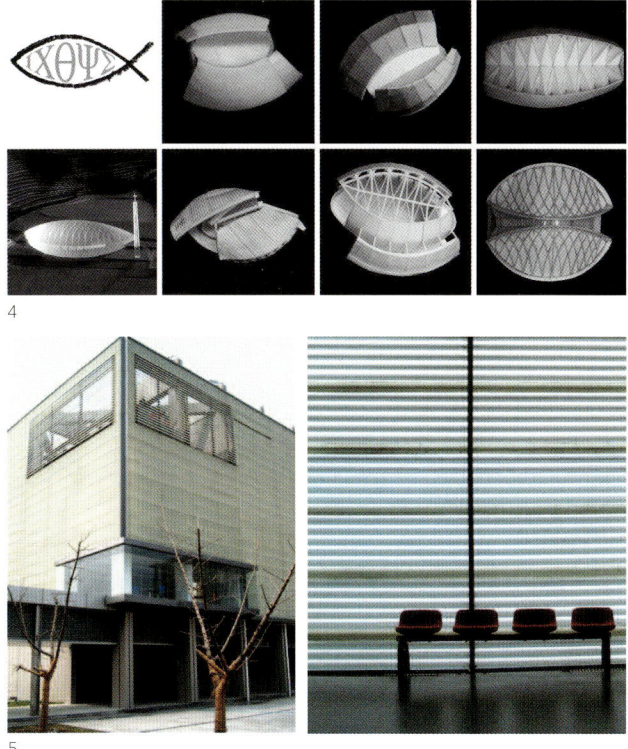

4

5

Similarly, J. J. Pan and Partners initiates discourse as the basis for refining and evolving the responsibility of architecture. In both the HTC R & D Project (Fig.3 & pp.198-201) and the ZyXEL R & D Campus in Wuxi (Fig.5 & pp.34-41), the discourse between interior and exterior, visibility and privacy challenge the theoretical definition and practical limits of building façades, pushing the architecture beyond stagnant

Irrigation waterway

Carved-in riverbed texture

Borders

Pebbles

Mosaic

Topographic analogy of the building form

6

engineers. J. J. Pan and Partners' fluency in architectural discourse goes beyond traditional Chinese culture. The Stockholm Library competition project (Fig.2 & pp.194-197) exemplifies the firm's expertise as an international architectural firm, through an intuitive understanding of foreign customs and translating them into celebrated designs.

On a conceptual level, discourse also embodies an informative journey. For the 2004 design competition of the Church of Suang-Lien Center for the Elderly (pp.154-163), in addition to challenges from prerequisite programmatic requirements and site complications, the distinctively identifiable "ΙΧΘΥΣ" theme (Fig.4) from Biblical scriptures became an inspiration which manifested throughout the design process, as a gesture for spatial rhetoric.

boundaries. The National Taichung Digital Library (Fig.6 & pp.220-225) highlights J. J. Pan and Partners' fluency with the urban milieu by envisioning the building as a civic capacitor, incorporating a fluid program, unconventional to its typology that encourages permeability across the platforms of urban space, people, and information.

On the external level, professionalism to J. J. Pan and Partners refers to taking on social responsibilities in the proficient execution of projects and provision of intellectual statements on design thinking. Internally, J. J. Pan and Partners defines professionalism as maintaining the highest level of technical competence with the best trained professionals. Therefore, the first step to the success of any project is the orchestration of fluid teams of designers and professionals with various backgrounds and expertise to allow crossover of disciplines, and empowering the task force with sufficient flexibility and efficiency to execute projects.

The firm believes in flexibility and diversity in its team structures; however, allowing team members to "grow with the project" is equally essential in securing teamwork

mentality, while also maintaining individualistic design freedom. Thus, key designers who contributed to the initial concept formation and brainstorming of the design parti are normally retained throughout the design phases. For instance, on the MediaTek Headquarters project (Fig.7 & pp.78-89), a newly graduated designer continued working on the project after concept and schematic design to personally develop professional skills in detailing and construction documents while assuring the project stayed true to its original concept.

Adopting new information technology, sophisticated building materials and advanced techniques in construction is the only

7

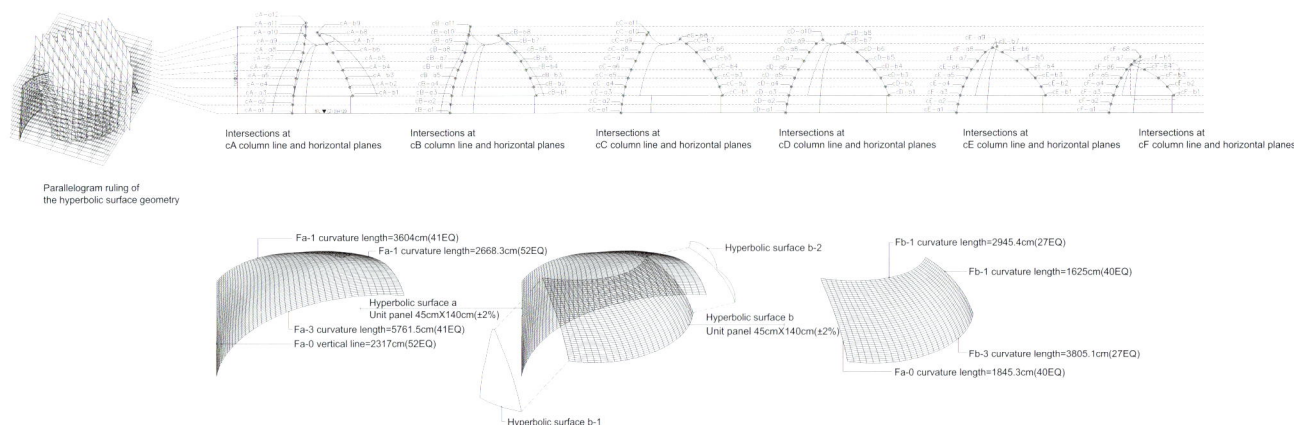

8

9

way to guarantee design innovation. Utilizing contemporary digital modeling techniques has not only given new forms to architecture, but has also allowed freedom in the construction methodologies. The enclosure and interior cladding of Church of Suang-Lien Center for the Elderly (Fig.8 & pp.154-163) represented J. J. Pan and Partners' first digitalized freeform construction documentation. Subsequently, the flowing façade of National Taichung Digital Library (Fig.9 & pp.220-225) and the folded skin at Neo Solar Power Office Building

(Fig.10 & pp.134-139) both illustrated how state-of-the-art design technology has become integral in manifesting the innovation and creativity of the architects.

In addition to mastering the balance between discourse and professionalism, J. J. Pan and Partners has always believed that sustainable design leads to sustainable practice. Leadership in ecological preservation and sustainable design is a critical component of our modus operandi as Taiwan's largest architectural firm. Dating back to the mid-1980s, the office had already gained recognition for our thorough and intuitive understanding of energy-efficient strategies and high-performance solutions. This environmental sensitivity commonly serves as a benchmark in J. J. Pan's daily design practice.

Relevant highlights include the active double-skin curtain wall design for the Kingyorker Headquarters project (Fig.11 & pp.42-47) set a precedent for Taiwan's building code in the

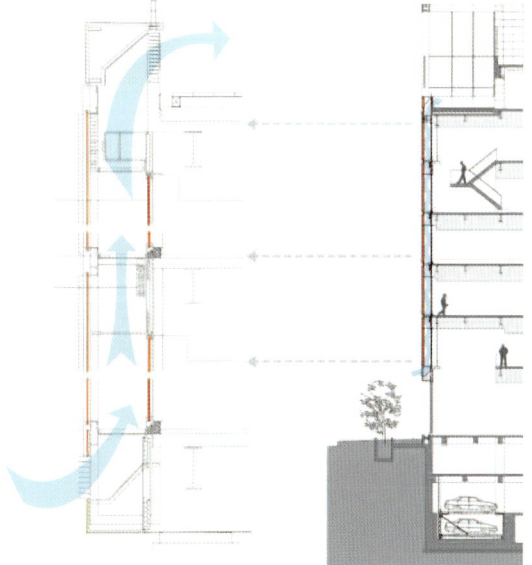

10   11

interpretation of local building industry standards. Furthermore, partnering with a highly progressive client in TSMC afforded us opportunities to combine a high-efficiency building envelope with both passive design strategies and high-tech sustainable features. The building (Fig.12,13 & pp.52-57) became the first office/fabrication building type to simultaneously achieve LEED Gold Certification in the US and EEWH Diamond Certificate in Taiwan.

J. J. Pan and Partners' comprehensive range of services translates to experience in a multitude of project types. Not only are the principles of "reduce, reuse and recycle" pertinent to our design approaches, but also the adaptation of historical buildings with innovative reuse, as exemplified in the Horizon Design Shanghai Office Project (Fig.14,15 & pp.22-33), which clearly demonstrated the firm's attitude towards sustainable design. The project transformed a once desolate factory into an award-winning office space and in the process sets a refreshing example for adaptive reuse.

In conclusion, the three components of "Yì" — sustainability, professionalism, and discourse — have laid a strong foundation for J. J. Pan. However, similar to how the character itself has evolved, "the arts" have shifted from an elite pursuit, to the diverse formats that permeate our contemporary lifestyle. As practitioners of the most practical of all Arts forms, architects now face an unprecedented range of challenges and responsibilities. In this regard, ancient wisdom in the form of Confucius' scripture offers invaluable guidance. Mr. Pan reinterprets a famous scripture as "Architecture as a practice

12

13

of art has to be in harmony with its environment, challenge and exceed conventions while respecting humanistic principles; then the architect can enjoy freedom in design." This simple yet profound ideal has been realized into magnificence throughout 30 years of practice at J. J. Pan. As our practice launches into the fourth decade, we pledge to think above and beyond the paradigm of the arts to contemplate the deeper meaning of our design and creativity.

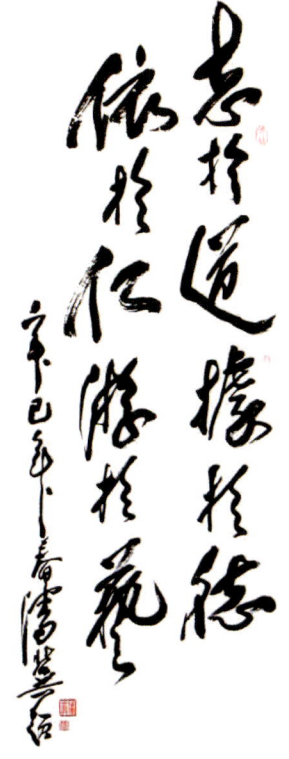

Set your heart upon the way
Base yourself on integrity
Lean upon Goodness and Virtue
Enjoy free spirit in the arts

Verse 6, Book 7 of The Analects of Confucius

14

15

Sustainability

Horizon Design
Shanghai Office

Design/Completion: 2005/2005
Shanghai, China
700 square meters
2008: AIA New York State Award of
Excellence for Adaptive Reuse
2008: The 2nd *Business Week/Architectural
Record* China Award for Best
Historic Preservation Project

Horizon Design's Shanghai office is situated in the Yangpu Creative Industrial Park, within Shanghai's old industrial zone along Yang Shu Pu Road. The historic factory site was originally constructed in 1921 and served as one of General Electric's largest manufacturing facilities in Asia throughout the early 20th century. During its occupation of Shanghai in WWII, the Japanese military used the building as an arsenal. After 1949 and until the end of the last century, the site was the workshop for the Shanghai Power Company. The building, having witnessed Shanghai's industrial development, is of significant historical value.

The renovations create a symbiosis between the historic and modern elements of the building, breathing new life into the structure by preserving the traces of the different ages and by revealing its historical and vernacular characteristics. The original factory walls, sash windows, steel truss and roofing have all been waterproofed and include a newly installed mechanical system. The work space— composed of offices, studios, conference rooms and a library—is enclosed in a series of "mini-environments" of various shapes to conserve energy. These "buildings within a building" help shape another order of spaces under a single roof, interacting with each other to initiate a dialogue between the "old" and "new" elements as an analogy of streets, plaza and building blocks in a city.

The iron floor plate and other recycled materials, unearthed during construction, are utilized in the new spaces to recall the vanishing craftsmanship of traditional industrial buildings.

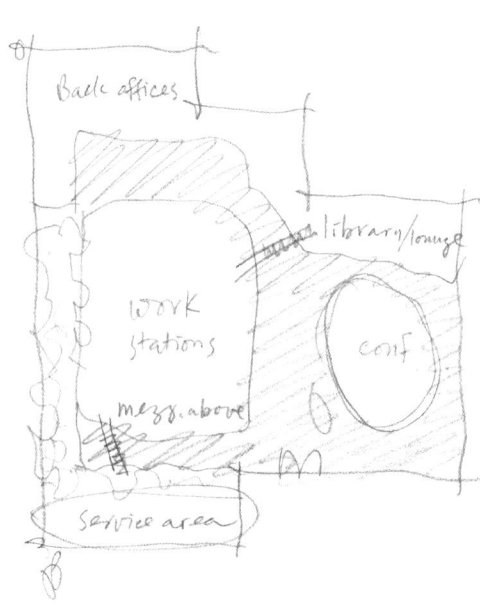

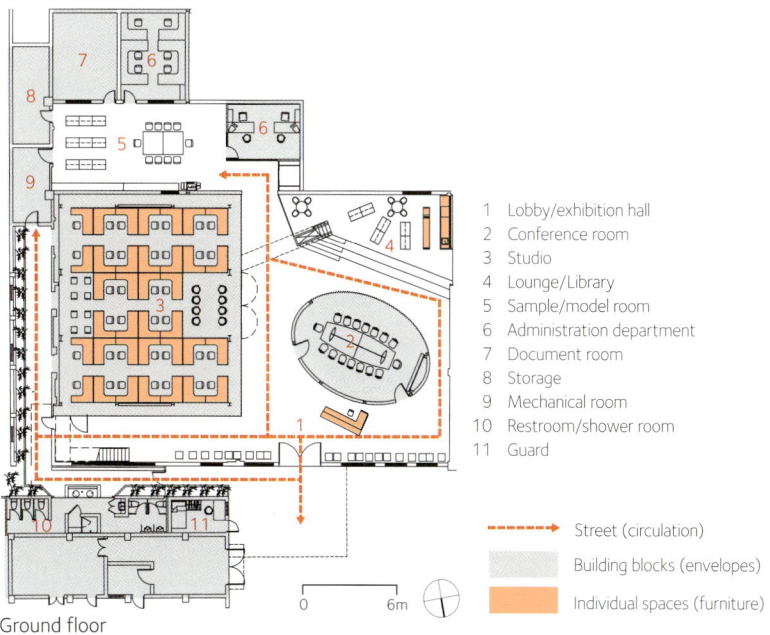

1 Lobby/exhibition hall
2 Conference room
3 Studio
4 Lounge/Library
5 Sample/model room
6 Administration department
7 Document room
8 Storage
9 Mechanical room
10 Restroom/shower room
11 Guard

- - -▶ Street (circulation)

 Building blocks (envelopes)

 Individual spaces (furniture)

0   6m

Ground floor

The conference room forms an elliptical shape with a solid wall made of locally reclaimed bricks. Its textured layering also serves as a backdrop to the reception area. On the other side of the conference room, a triangular stage constructed of recovered wood planks serves as the staff lounge and doubles as a library. For major events, the conference room's translucent partitions can be disassembled to provide a visual and physical connection between the library and conference room.   The full-height glass partitions wrapping the studio spaces help alleviate the pressure from the roof's massive volume. A lightweight steel stair neatly connecting the studio to the mezzanine above also helps keep the historical roof structure intact and accessible.

The oval conference room made of reclaimed bricks: Various tones lend the wall texture and highlight the historical nature of the space.

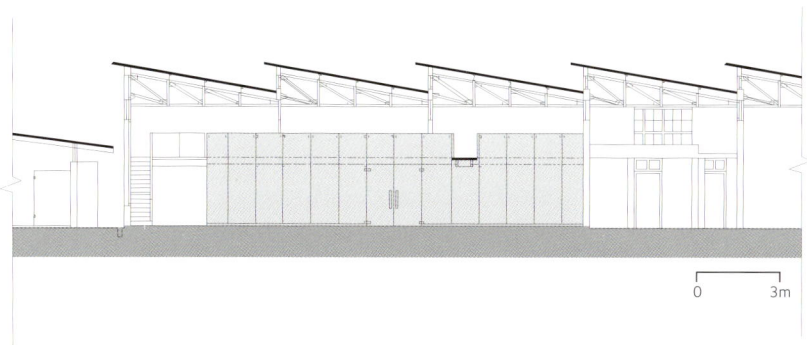

Secional elevation at Studio

Customized furniture design to meet special demands of individual spaces

1   Structural steel beam
2   TH5mm steel plate @ 45cm
3   45° polished edges
4   Bracket
5   Laminated glass support
6   Laminated glass
7   Steel holder with M12 sockets
8   Steel plate
9   Transparent sealant
10 Stainless steel base

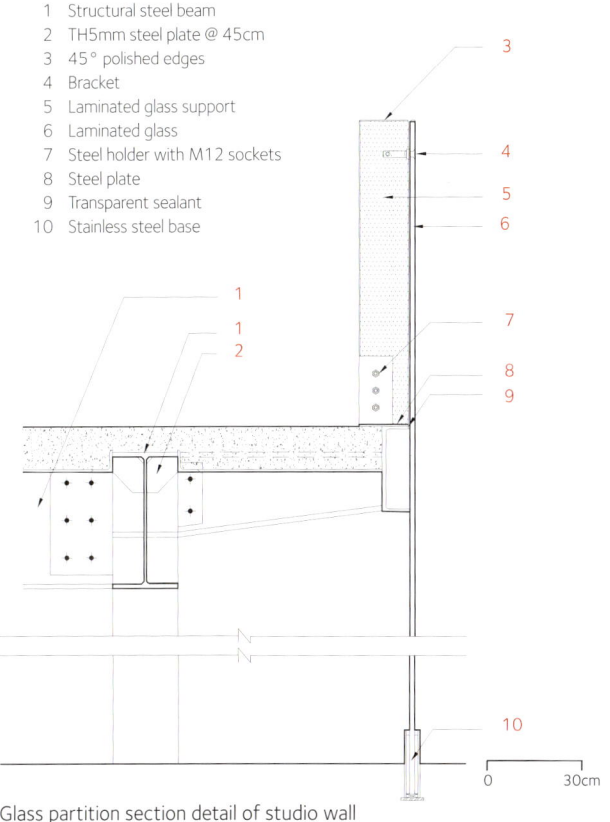

Glass partition section detail of studio wall

0   30cm

Horizon Design has set an exemplary precedent through its adaptive reuse of an old industrial building by respecting and preserving the essence of historical spaces so as to maintain a dialogue between the old and the new.

ZyXEL R & D Campus

Design/Completion: 2002/2004
Jiangsu, China
36,410 square meters

The Wuxi R & D campus for ZyXEL Corporation, a global leader in communication technology, consists of a technology center, a dormitory and a gymnasium.

The newly established facilities are remote from the hometowns of most employees; hence the biggest design challenge posed was creating a perfectly balanced environment for work, recreation, and the incorporation of private living for the employees. The compact campus is shaped by three buildings configured around the central greenery. Corridors between the buildings establish transitional spaces from work to recreation and exercise facilities, and finally to the quiet sleeping zone.

At the gymnasium, the innovative use of fiber-reinforced corrugated plastic sheeting, an affordable building material commonly used as lightweight roofing, not only provides the indoor sports court with ample daylight, but also enriches the façade with its fluted texture and lantern-like lighting effect at night. At the dormitory, providing residents with undisturbed private living space was the greatest concern for the designers. This design challenge was solved through the use of operable grill windows, resembling classical wood carving shutters in traditional Chinese residences, to screen off sight lines between opposite rooms. Natural light illuminates the interior and casts shadows against the wooden grill boxes, continuously transforming the atmosphere in the atrium throughout the changing seasons.

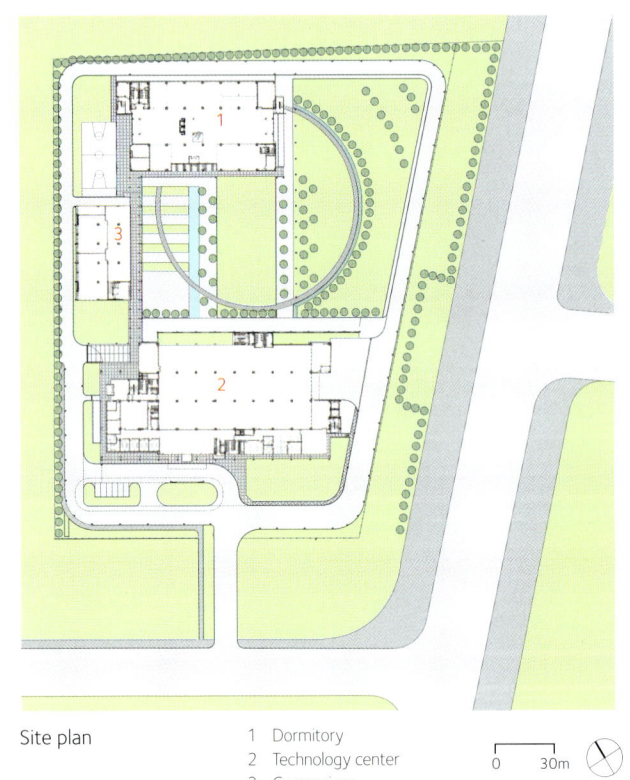

Site plan

1 Dormitory
2 Technology center
3 Gymnasium

0   30m

The landscape design is a duet between sense and rationality. The circular path cuts through the linear landscape elements and serves as a link between the office and the dormitory. The open space is defined by tall trees along the curved edge of the lawn. The walkway wound around shallow water provides a pleasant sense of casually strolling along the stepped-stone path.

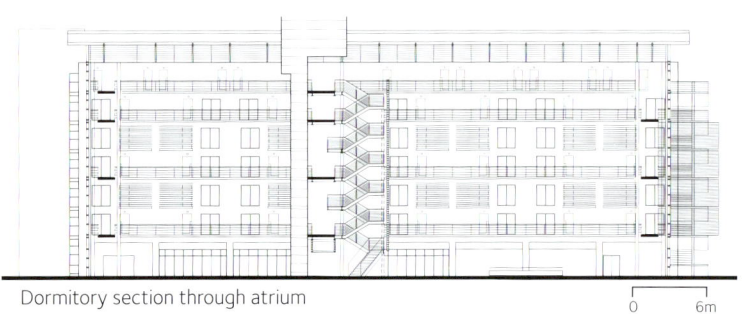

Dormitory section through atrium

0   6m

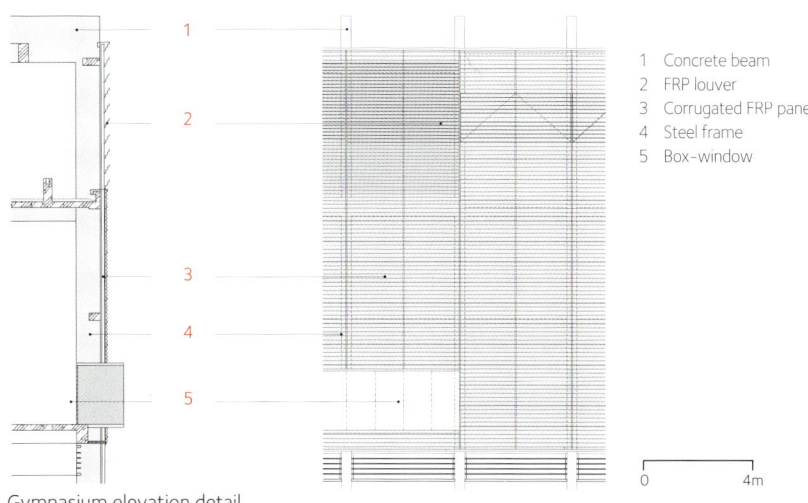

1 Concrete beam
2 FRP louver
3 Corrugated FRP panel
4 Steel frame
5 Box-window

Gymnasium elevation detail

Kingyorker Headquarters

Design/Completion: 2005/2008
Taipei
4380 square meters
2008: Taiwan Interior Design Award of Working Space

Situated in the Neihu Technology Park in Taipei, a newly developed high-tech office park that is already densely populated with flashy corporate headquarters, the building employs a simple façade as deliberate contrast to its busy context.

Structural efficiency plays a crucial role in this compact floor plan. A combined long and short-span column grid working in conjunction with the integrated seismic damper in the stair core successfully achieves a column-free interior space to meet the requirement of maximum open office area for planning flexibility and efficiency.

Sustainable design features include: double-skin glazed facades with active heat gain reduction and insulation capability, and an automated sunshade on the western façade. The advanced double wall system also sets a precedent for building code interpretation of floor area and mechanical system design in Taiwan, consequently promoting the future use of such systems.

A green roof on the seventh floor helps reduce heat gain while providing a "green island" in an urban environment. The private lounge with circular reflective granite seating located at the entrance mirrors the bamboo groves on the roof garden, subtly hinting at the enterprise's Asian characteristics.

BRB
Image from Taiwan NCREE

Steel casing
In-fill concrete
Unbonding layer

Core steel

Steel framing system with large span composite beams creates column-free office space. Patented ductile buckling restrain brace (BRB) on the service core plays a major role as the lateral system of seismic design.

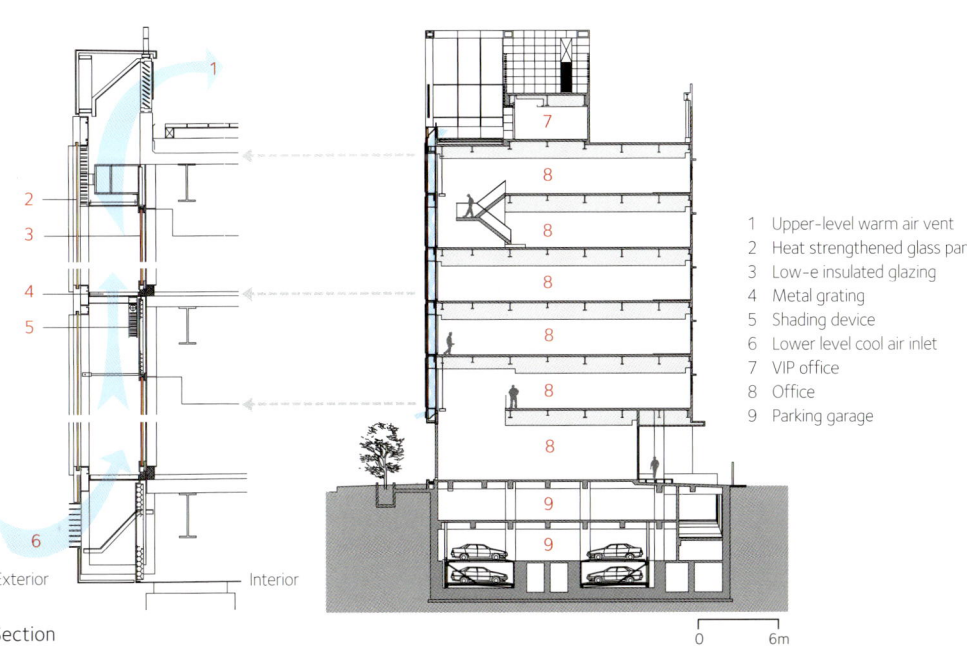

1 Upper-level warm air vent
2 Heat strengthened glass panel
3 Low-e insulated glazing
4 Metal grating
5 Shading device
6 Lower level cool air inlet
7 VIP office
8 Office
9 Parking garage

Exterior   Interior

Section

0   6m

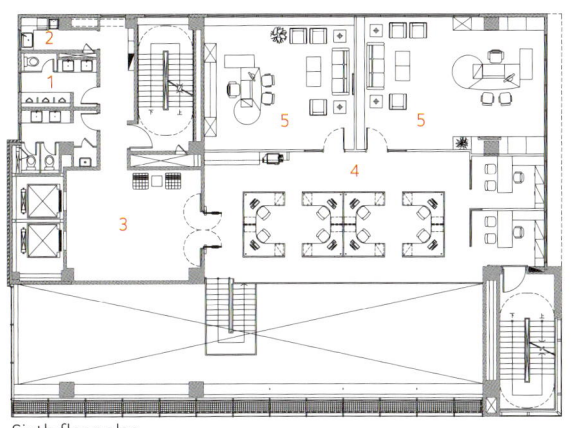

Sixth floor plan

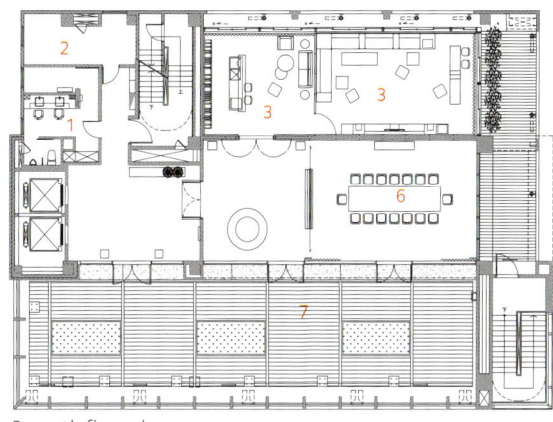

Seventh floor plan

1 Restrooms
2 Kitchenette
3 Lounge
4 Working area
5 Executive office
6 Conference room
7 Terrace/garden

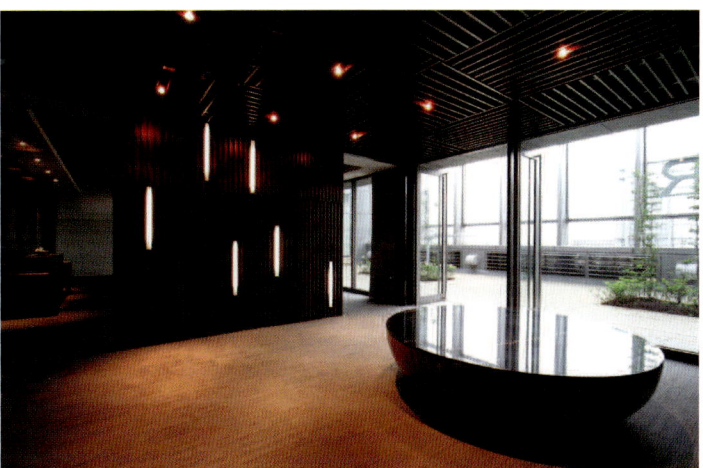

The circular granite block serves as a metaphor for a reflection pond that blends the exterior roof garden with the interior lounge.

Taipei Street Furniture Design

Design/Completion: 2005/2007
Taipei
Thirteen major bus routes

Conventionally, the design of street furniture in Taiwan falls under the category of industrial design. Most public agencies therefore design street furniture from a purely economic and functional perspective, while aesthetics and the urban context are barely taken into consideration. The office of J. J. Pan and Partners, however, was commissioned by the Build-Operate-Transfer (BOT) contractor to design a collection of street furniture that had to be aesthetically pleasing as well as functional, incorporating a unique theme that illustrates the city's vibrant contemporary culture.

The new collection of street furniture includes bus stop shelters, advertisement panels, poster columns, benches, bicycle racks, bus stop posts and trash cans. The project was implemented in 2006 by an advertising agency working for the City of Taipei as a part of the BOT package.

 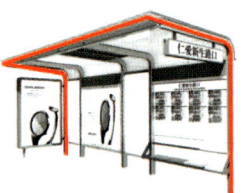      

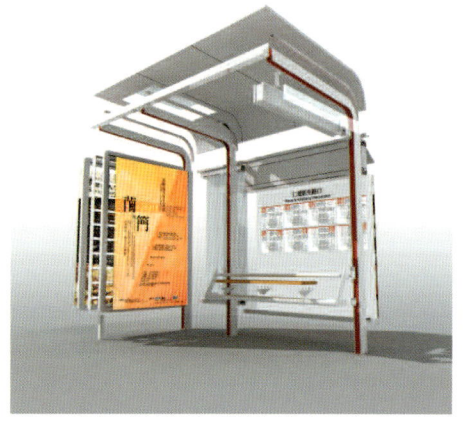

The street furniture designed by J. J. Pan and Partners invokes a dialogue between the hectic street atmosphere and the simple, humble style of modern furniture. By adopting neutral colors and simple forms, the street furniture stands out from the complicated urban context with a subdued clarity. The sleek outline of the extruded aluminum frames featuring a simple, curved "cloud-like" theme is derived from classical Ming Dynasty style furniture. As a reminder of the graceful bent wood craftsmanship commonly seen in traditional Chinese furniture, the distinctive curves appear repeatedly on various furniture in different sizes, emphasizing the beauty of design integration while contrasting with the busy surroundings.

For the ease of construction and assembly, lightweight aluminum frames with prefabricated joints not only make shipping and on-site installation efficient but also increase durability. Details of rounded corners and edges help reduce day-to-day maintenance load while adapting to users' comfort. Modulated honeycomb panels reduce bus shelter heat transmission and project a sense of simplicity. Only sustainable materials were used in the construction of the street furniture, being either recyclable or recycled—namely aluminum, tempered glass and synthetic wood studs.

To meet the expectations of the Municipality, the collection of new street furniture carries design elements that incorporate domestic cultural insignias blended with unique contemporary images. From the passenger's perspective along the tree-shaded sidewalks of Taipei, the shadow of leaves cast over the translucent pattern of classical wooden shutter printing on the sunroof creates an intriguing composition.

Just as a piece of antique furniture in a living room reflects the owner's taste, Taipei's street furniture, through its modern interpretation of classical inspired forms, subtly reminds people of the elegance of contemporary civilian urban life.

Bike rack detail

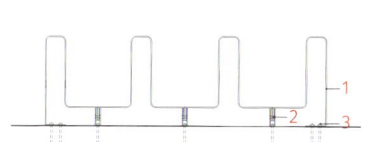

1 Flat stainless steel plate
  (sand blasted surface)
2 Bolt lock
3 Expansion anchor bolt

TSMC Fab 12, Phase 4

Design/Completion: 2006/2009
Hsinchu Science Park, Taiwan
276,090 square meters

TSMC is one of the world's largest dedicated semiconductor foundries offering leading wafer process technologies. With the construction of the Fab 12, Phase 4 expansion, four principles of architectural design—congeniality, interaction, transparency and sustainability—are highlighted to further elaborate the original corporate identity system of environmental responsibility.

In accordance with the massing of existing headquarters across the major access road, the site plan allows for a balanced building volume along both sides of the street. Efficiency in functional layout and construction cost is meticulously assessed by utilizing building information models to achieve optimum floor layout. As the size of the building increases to accommodate higher rates of productivity, between-floor travel distance for staff becomes a more complex issue in office planning. For example, stairs are placed between floors to receive while natural lighting to brighten the surrounding spaces.

To minimize environmental impact, green design, construction methods and materials are effectively utilized to improve the site's sustainability, raise energy efficiency and reduce negative effects on the ecosystem. The setbacks along neighboring sites are designed as an ecological water channel, increasing the biological diversity and restoring the natural environment. In addition, green roofs and the use of light colors on the exterior of the building enclosure increase thermal insulation and reduce heat islanding, therefore cutting down total energy demand on the cooling system.

Upholding the principles of green construction at each concept and design stage saw this project achieve EEWH Diamond and LEED Gold certification in 2009.

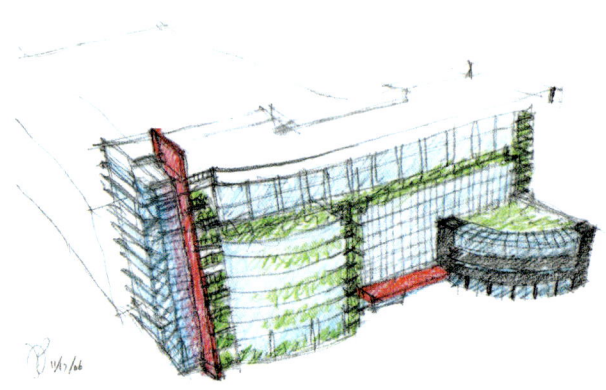
Sketch of early scheme

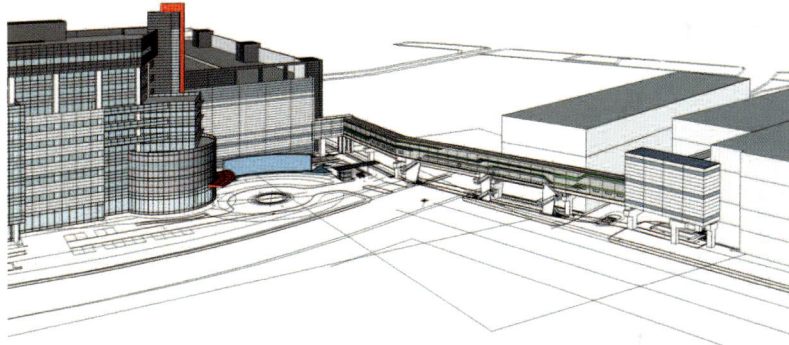

One of the significant breakthroughs in this project was the application of the enclosed bridge linking the buildings to transport materials within a controlled environment.

The ecological water channel helps restore the biodiversity of the surrounding environment.

Test Research Inc. (TRI) Headquarters

Design/Completion: 2006/2008
Taoyuan, Taiwan
27,160 square meters
2008: Gold Plaque Award, Taoyuan Architecture
Award for Industrial/Commercial Building

Test Research Inc. is a leading solution provider for automated inspection and testing systems for the information and communications industries. Various functions of the project cluster harmoniously around an open courtyard, the result of a dual-phased development. The sunken garden, sheltered from the strong northeast seasonal wind, not only integrates the working areas above grade with the basement dining hall and fitness center but also extends views and activities into the landscaped outdoor space.

To enrich the modern, clean façade, warm-textured natural granite cladding is used instead of the flashy metal panels common to industrial buildings. The frames of the low-e glass window units are set flush with the stone exterior wall to give the building a clean, sharp image that requires minimal maintenance. Porches and balconies, defined by setbacks at the bottom and top floors, elaborate the precise composition of spaces, and initiate a dialogue between the building's expression and its surroundings. The corridor, with up-turned structural beams, achieves a slender visual effect.

1   Lobby
2   Canteen
3   Parking garage
4   Loading area
5   Water wall

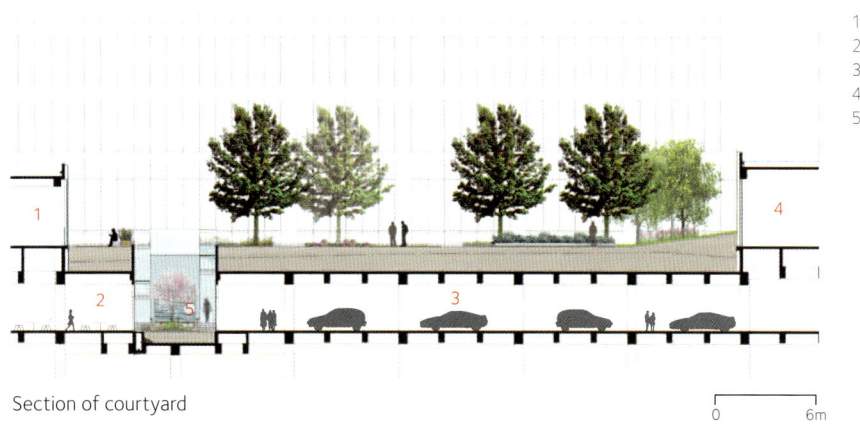

Section of courtyard

0   6m

The pavement on the courtyard and adjacent interior corridors is finished with the same granite as the building's exterior wall, giving the environment a harmonious look. Pebble infills help resolve odd-shaped gaps between the hard-paved plaza and the building's edge.

The landscape complements the floor plan's geometry and repetitive elements of the building. The shifting and undulating levels give the courtyard a tranquil atmosphere. Located at the center of the canteen, the linear atrium with fragrant plants becomes an extension of the ground-level garden. A picturesque three-tiered waterfall enhances the experience of traveling up and down the stairs by linking the ground level with the layered landscape.

In a thorough contemplation of the human-environment relationship, the architectural design of the project mitigates the rigid high-tech corporate image, and creates a friendly work environment.

1 Production area
2 Elevator lobby
3 Mechanical room

Typical floor plan

1 Production area
2 Conference room
3 Elevator lobby
4 Mechanical room
5 Bridge to phase II

Second floor plan

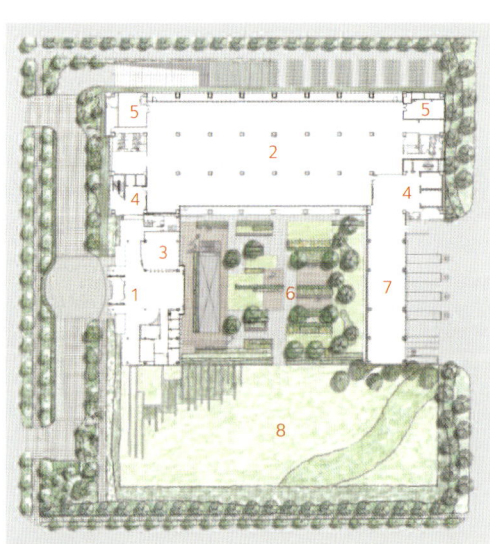

1 Lobby
2 Production area
3 Conference room
4 Elevator lobby
5 Mechanical room
6 Courtyard
7 Loading area
8 Reserved for future expansion

Ground floor plan

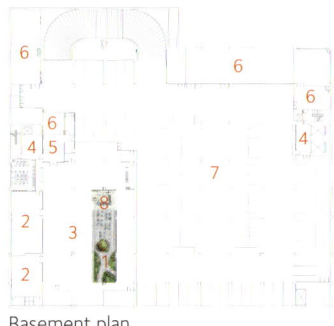

1 Sunken courtyard
2 Fitness room
3 Canteen
4 Elevator lobby
5 Lobby
6 Mechanical room
7 Parking garage
8 Water wall

0   20m

Basement plan

Section through sunken courtyard

0   3m

Dingpu MRT Station

Design/Completion: 2006/2013
Taipei

The design theme of the Dingpu MRT station, which serves as both the Tucheng line's terminus and the future Sanying line's starting station, differs from that of other stations. In response to the evolutionary transformation of Dingpu from an early industrial (coal) township into its present status as a technology center, historical context and contemporary urban flux have both been incorporated into the station's architectural design.

Serving as the end-point of an underground line connecting to a future elevated line, the interior of the station is analogous to the transient qualities of light in relation to time. The character "C", representing carbon, is adopted as a graphic icon, and implies the revolutionary progress from coal mines to high-tech carbon nanotubes.

The use of natural light as a sustainable design element also sets a precedent for subterranean transit stations in Taiwan. Sunlight is captured through a row of reflective solar tubes running the length of the station mezzanine. Accompanied by supplemental light fixtures, natural light from the collectors resembles vibrant sunbeams that create virtual atriums, intuitively guiding passengers through high traffic areas. During inclement weather, the collectors are shielded by transparent enclosures for protection.

Longitudinal section

1 Platform
2 Paid area
3 Passenger lobby
4 Staff area
5 Mechanical room
6 Light inducting shaft

0   20m

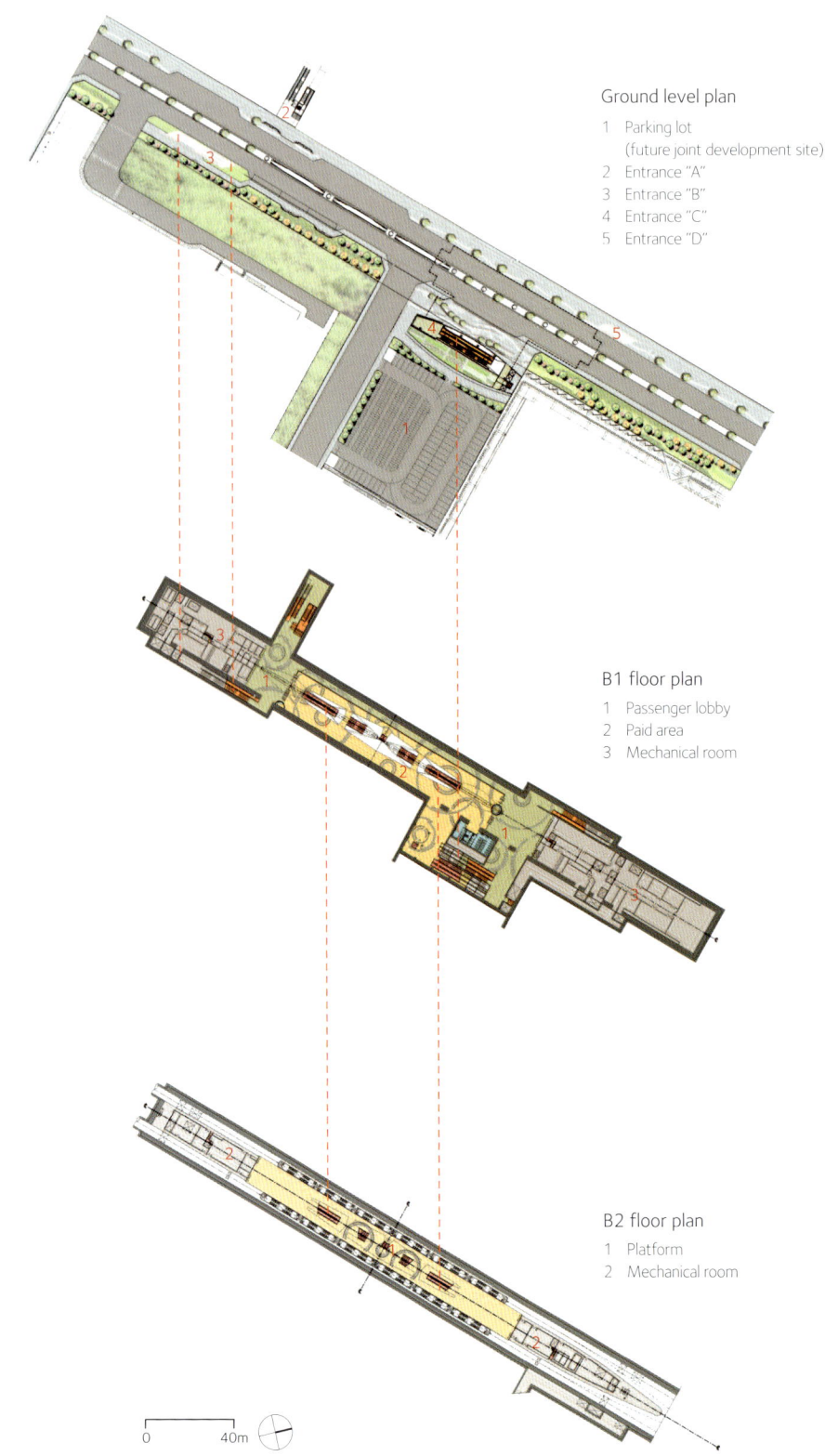

Ground level plan

1 Parking lot
(future joint development site)
2 Entrance "A"
3 Entrance "B"
4 Entrance "C"
5 Entrance "D"

B1 floor plan

1 Passenger lobby
2 Paid area
3 Mechanical room

B2 floor plan

1 Platform
2 Mechanical room

0   40m

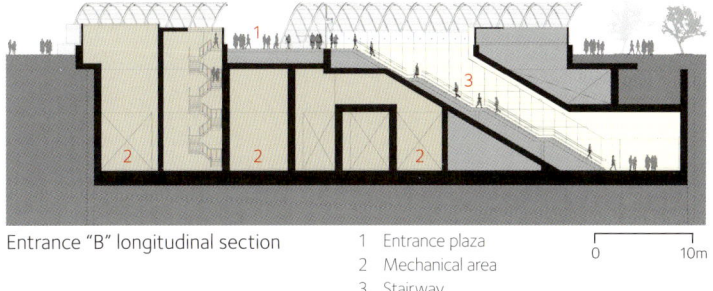

Entrance "B" longitudinal section

1 Entrance plaza
2 Mechanical area
3 Stairway

0   10m

Integrated lighting fixtures reinforce the design theme by abstractly expressing light waves, halos and radiancy, appearing as patterns on the ceiling, floor and walls. Ceiling panels are arranged in accordance with the floor pattern. Programmable colorful LED light fixtures embedded in the concourse wall poetically reflect the changing environment. The steel spiral tube structure at entrance "B" further strengthens the natural lighting effect with its transparent enclosure.

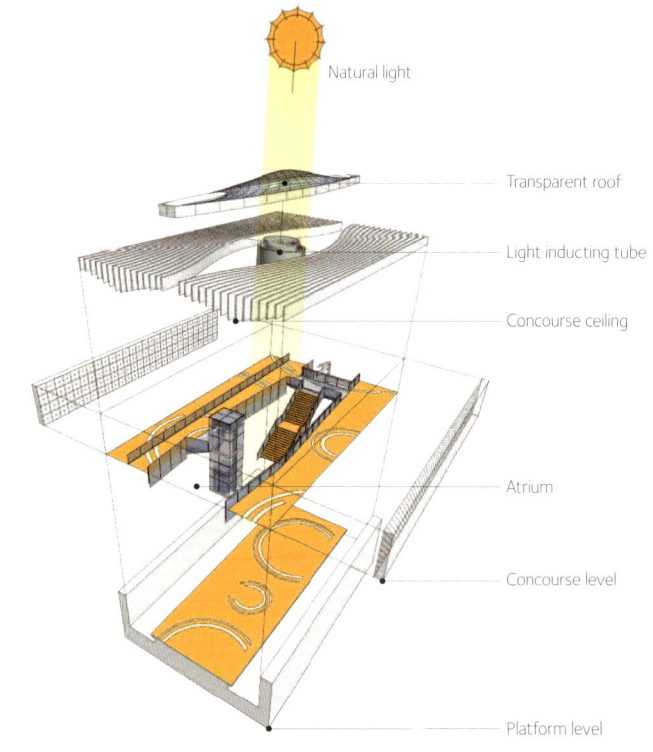

Natural light

Transparent roof

Light inducting tube

Concourse ceiling

Atrium

Concourse level

Platform level

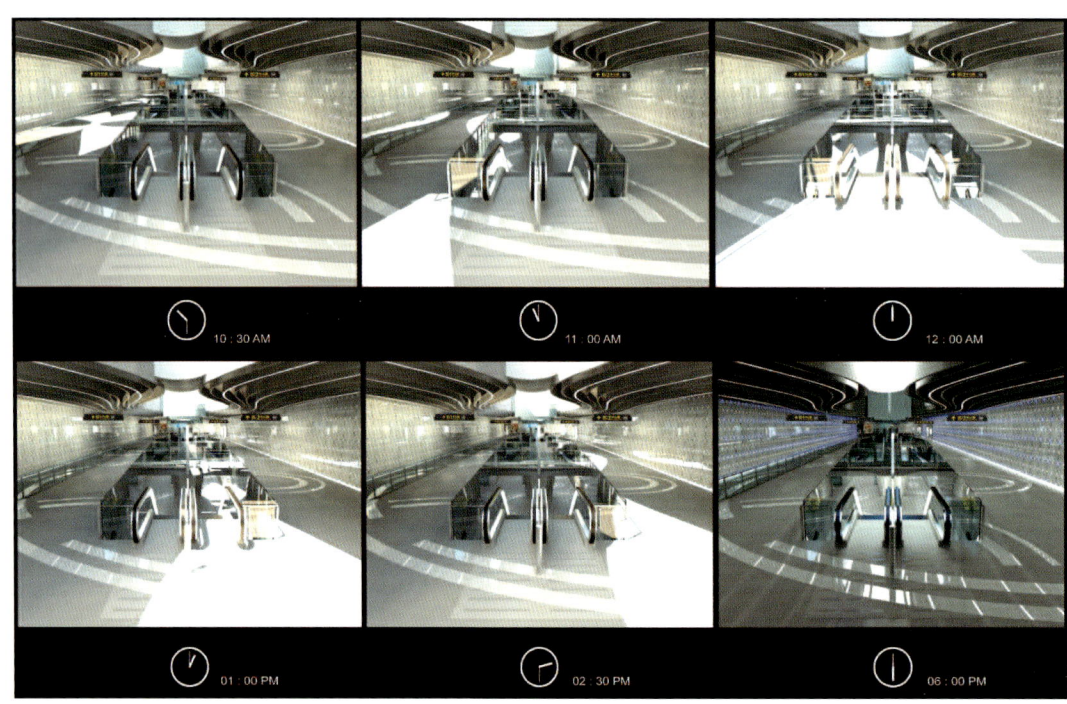

10 : 30 AM

11 : 00 AM

12 : 00 AM

01 : 00 PM

02 : 30 PM

06 : 00 PM

With the sunlight collectors bringing natural light to the interiors, the concourse level is a vibrant mix of ever-changing light and pedestrian flow.

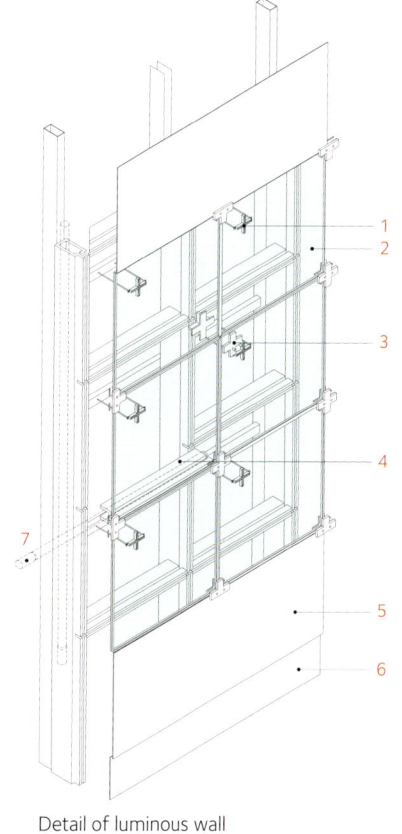

1 Cross light
2 Laminated glass
3 S.S cross pitch cover
4 Custom aluminum sash PVDF coating
5 A.L panel PVDF coating
6 S.S panel
7 Flexible LED light

0   60cm

Detail of luminous wall

Sanya Tropical Resort Hotel

Design/Completion: 2007/2012
Hainan, China
76,605 square meters

The Sanya Tropical Resort Hotel sits at the intersection of two major roadways entering downtown Sanya, a resort city in Hainan Province, China's largest tropical island province, famous for its expansive stretches of picturesque sandy beaches and mild weather all year round. Operating in a competitive market, the client expects this resort to set itself apart from other beach resorts through its unique features and thoughtful design.

Located inland, some distance from the scenic coastline, the resort hotel has to create attractions of its own to generate tourism as well as capitalize on the land value. The resort utilizes a water park theme to take advantage of the on-site underground hot springs. In order to maximize the privacy of the different programs while minimizing sightline interference, the high-rise hotel complex is sited to the south, facing the boulevard with landmark distinction, whereas the upscale guest suite clusters are located along the east and west boundaries of the triangular-shaped site. The hotel's double-loaded corridor layout allows for large fenestrations with views towards the exterior scene or the courtyard. The semi-outdoor terraces at the elevator lobbies introduce natural light and refreshing breezes to enhance the vacation atmosphere.

One of the most prominent features of the guest room design is the 10-meter-long private "sky pool" on each balcony. These elaborately designed private pools give each individual guest room in the high-rise tower a touch of the tropical resort lifestyle. Natural ventilation through the balcony, cooled by the sky pool water, further enhances the indoor air quality as well as energy efficiency.

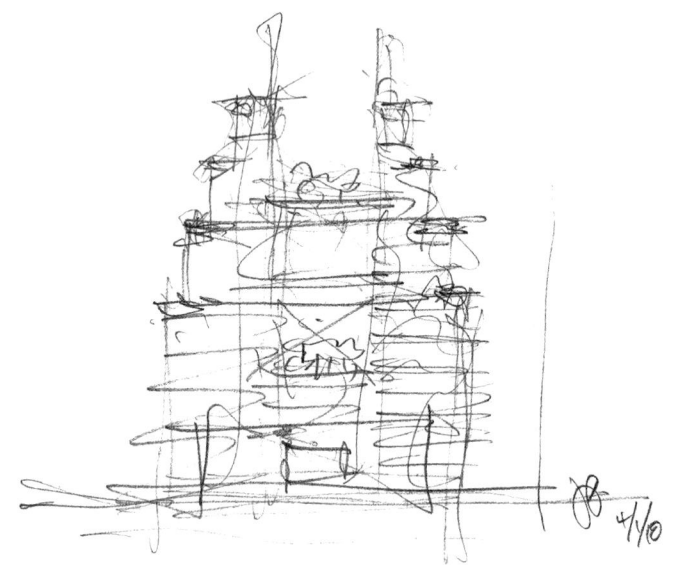

Shaped by the intensive program criteria and strict code requirements, the twin tower adopts a stepped outline resembling the profile of a traditional Balinese gateway to the temples. Vertical greenery on the façade is achieved through the placement of planter boxes at each level. Wooden grills outside the veranda frame views from the guest rooms while screening off exterior-mounted mechanical equipment. Operable doors and windows along the guest rooms' and reception lobby's deep balcony recess allow for natural ventilation and the penetration of natural light throughout the day. Well designed architectural details make the resort compatible with the vernacular environment while the carefully selected finishing materials and color schemes enhance the local tropical island theme.

The guest suites fully integrate with the surroundings through the use of green roofs for their energy-conserving insulation and water-retention properties. All the waste water from the resort is treated through a water-recycling biotope and can be reused to irrigate the gardens and the green roofs. The outdoor landscaped gardens, lush with indigenous plants and ecological ponds, exemplify the project's sensitivity to Hainan's natural environment.

Site plan

1 Lobby
2 Restaurant
3 Shop
4 Office
5 Lounge bar
6 Clubhouse
7 Hot spring area
8 Guest suites
9 Villa

0   48m

Section elevation

1 Guestrooms
2 Lobby
3 Restaurant
4 Clubhouse
5 Guest suites

0   20m

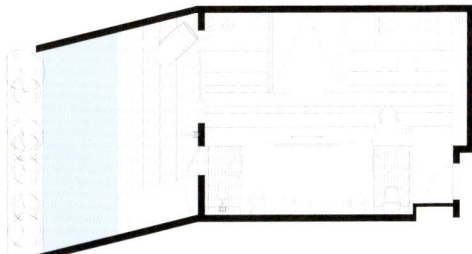

Typical guest room plan

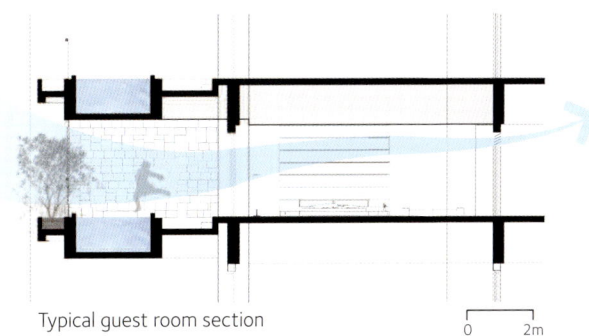

Typical guest room section

0   2m

Professionalism

MediaTek Headquarters

Design/Completion: 2003/2005
Hsinchu Science Park, Taiwan
150,000 square meters

The headquarters for MediaTek, a creative micro-electronic design corporation, consolidates its global operations, research labs, design houses, and conference and training facilities on a 3-hectare site facing an 80-meter-wide greenbelt in northern Taiwan.

The layout of the headquarters reflects the specific needs of a fabless semiconductor business. The floor plans for two major functional groups—the headquarters' offices and the design houses—contain distinct planning features. The stepped building envelopes and alternating rooftop terraces for the design houses are customized to accommodate the unique organization and working pattern of each research lab. The "hand-shaped" layout stretching towards the greenbelt maximizes views for each individual design lab without interrupting one another. The curvilinear shape of the glass curtain wall helps reduce the pressure placed on the side of the building facing the main street by the tower's massive volume.

Comfort in the working environment is further improved through the introduction of ample natural light and greenery in the office. An innovative tensile structural system achieves a column-free dining hall with spectacular views through its 50-meter-long glazed façade fronting the greenbelt.

The auditorium, with its curved slatted wall inside a transparent enclosure, was conceived as a second vantage point along the main street. The main entrance of the building is oriented towards the south to counteract the strong northeasterly seasonal wind. The reception hall's concave metal roof echoes the curvature of the headquarters' curtain wall as a welcoming gesture to celebrate the sense of arrival. The pavement alternates with green landscapes to accommodate the diverse function of each different sector at the rectilinear entrance plaza.

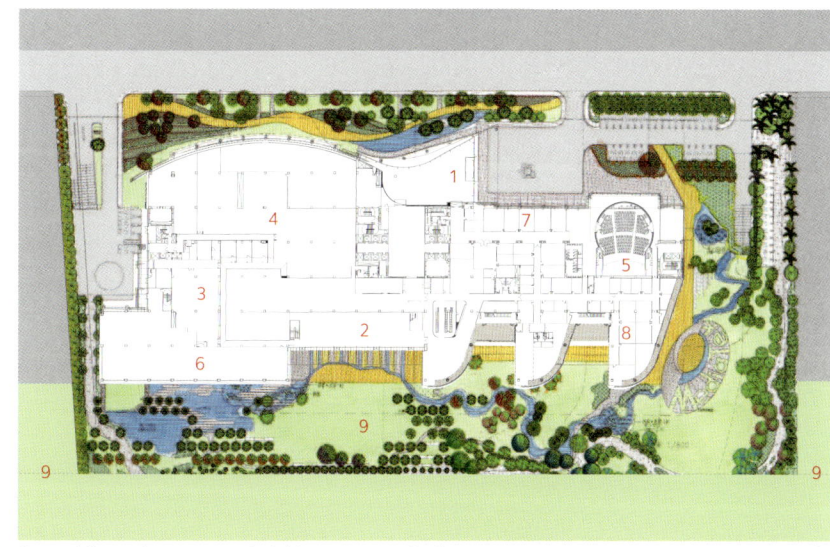

Ground floor plan

1 Lobby
2 Canteen
3 Pantry
4 Testing area
5 Auditorium

6 Fitness center
7 Conference rooms
8 Office
9 80-meter greenbelt setback

0   30m

The visual focus of the northern façade is the auditorium; expressed as a distinct circular element with vertical metal cladding that contrasts with the horizontal mullions of the rectangular glass enclosure.

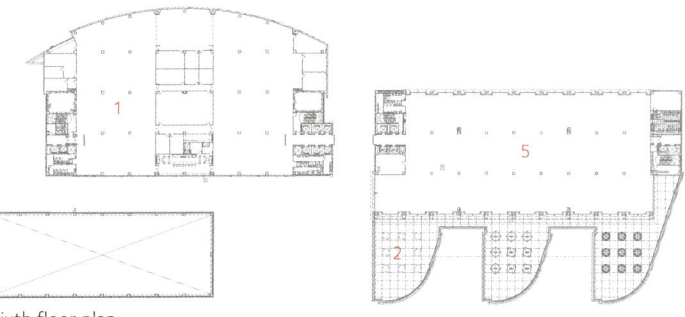

Sixth floor plan

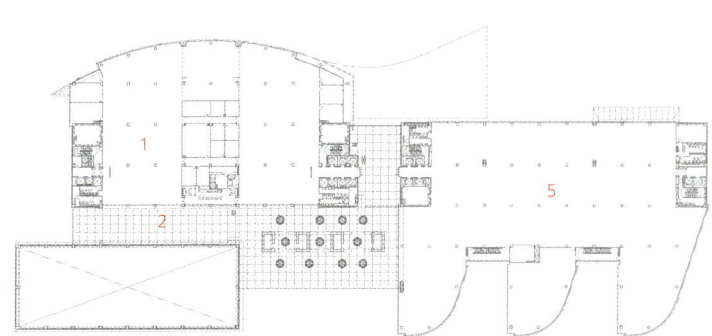

Third floor plan

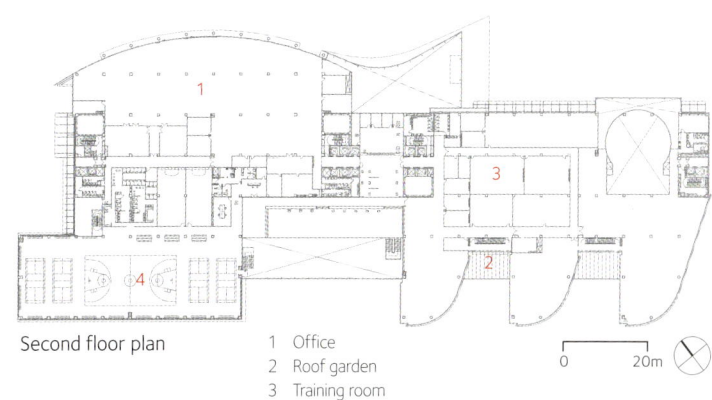

Second floor plan

1 Office
2 Roof garden
3 Training room
4 Gymnasium
5 Design house

0   20m

Detail at steel rod connection

Section details

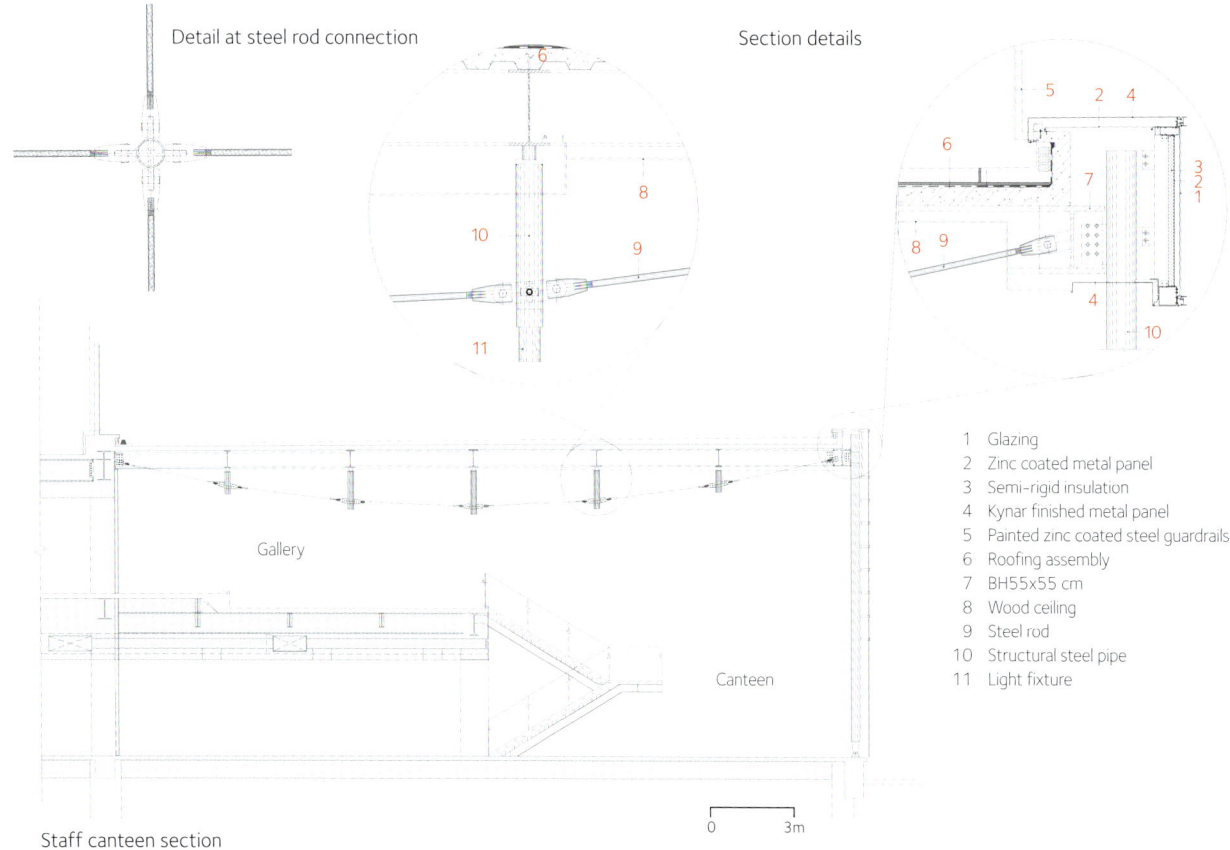

6

5 2 4

8

6

7

10

3
2
1

9

8 9

7

11

4

10

Gallery

Canteen

1   Glazing
2   Zinc coated metal panel
3   Semi-rigid insulation
4   Kynar finished metal panel
5   Painted zinc coated steel guardrails
6   Roofing assembly
7   BH55x55 cm
8   Wood ceiling
9   Steel rod
10 Structural steel pipe
11 Light fixture

Staff canteen section

0   3m

The "open-hand" configuration of the design houses employs curvilinear southern façades that maximize views of the 80-meter-wide greenbelt.

Lien Hwa Headquarters

Design/Completion: 2005/2009
Taipei
52,250 square meters

The completion of the high-speed rail and MRT system has transformed Taipei's Nangang District from a traditional industrial suburb into a thriving bio-technology and information technology hub. The site, located on the border of the Nangang Software Park and the National Exhibition and Convention Center, plays an important role in its regional development.

With the railway tracks at the rear of the site removed, the site consequently borders two main streets along its north and south sides. In response to this double-frontage site feature, the planning strategy called for a modest mid-rise twin tower scheme that would fit the surroundings, rather than an out-of-context high-rise single tower approach.

The placement of the two buildings at opposite corners of the site initiates a conversation between the towers and the surrounding context. A sky bridge linking the two buildings at the podium helps define the hierarchy of outdoor spaces and extends the urban fabric into the courtyard. The service cores of each building are strategically located against the east and west sides of the building with their solid façades blocking out heat gain from extensive exposure to sunlight. Optimal visual effect and shading efficiency have been achieved through careful examination of curtain wall mock-ups and sun angle studies.

The interior office space is a representation of the exterior architecture. The hammered finish, solid granite lobby wall in tower A, symbolizes the enterprise's traditional industrious spirit—"honest, simple, studious, and prudent." On the other hand, gray slate and metallic finished panels in tower B echo the spirit of the innovative high-tech industry.

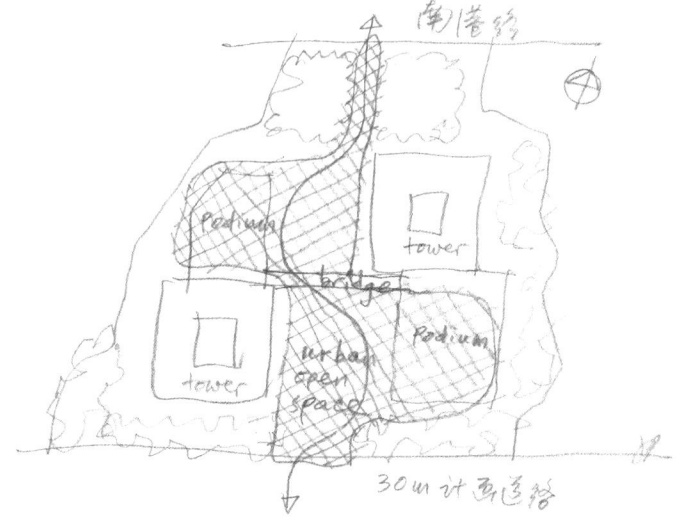

The sky bridge facilitates movements between the LH headquarters and its subsidiary while keeping their respective privacy.

The concentric circular pattern centering on the entrances of both buildings leads to the theme of landscape design. Elements such as pavings, tree holes and planter boxes are coherently linked by water features.

The garden on the fourth floor includes a bar, a waterfall and stacked rocks, creating a casual atmosphere. The wooden decks and stage in front of the waterfall provide a spacious outdoor reception area. A continuation of the ground floor plaza, the basement courtyard evokes a sense of tranquility. A subtle transition of ambient light is cast through fritted patterns on the glass curtain wall to give the building a landmark highlight, and to give the city a spectacle of glamor and hospitality.

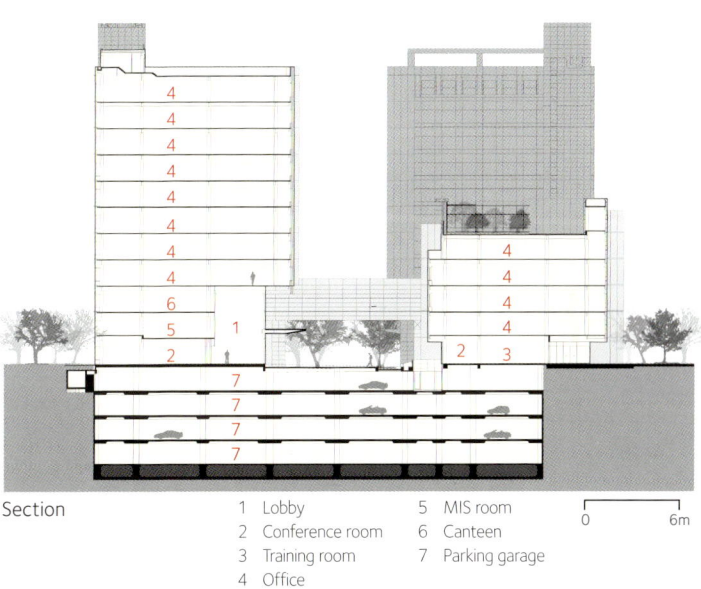

Section

1 Lobby
2 Conference room
3 Training room
4 Office
5 MIS room
6 Canteen
7 Parking garage

0   6m

1 Lobby
2 Showroom
3 Conference room
4 Mechanical room
5 Training room
6 Auditorium
7 Preparation room

Building A

Building B

Ground floor plan

0   20m

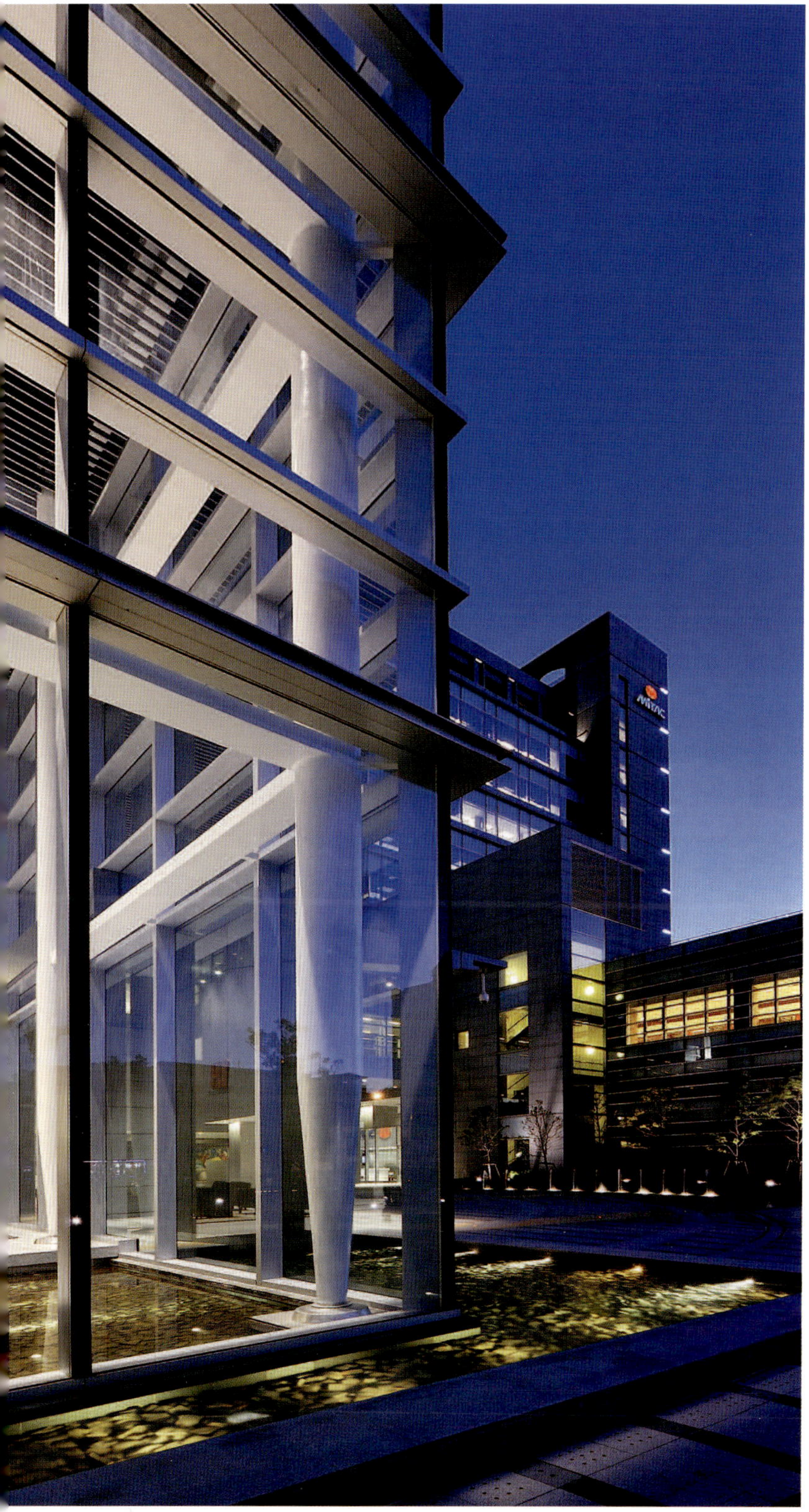

Section at Building A lobby

4FL

3FL

2FL

Ground-floor
showroom

1FL

0   2m

1 Private lounge
2 VIP lounge
3 Kitchen
4 Conference room
5 Mechanical room
6 Office
7 Roof garden

11th floor plan

1 Office
2 Mechanical room
3 Founder's memorial hall
4 Roof garden

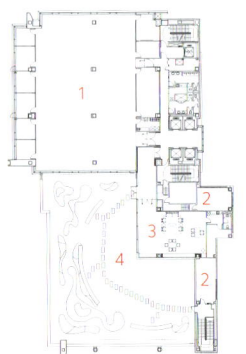

Sixth floor plan

1 Office
2 Mechanical room
3 Fitness center
4 Sky bridge
5 Canteen
6 Pantry

Third floor plan

0   20m

A rooftop garden set in the middle of the 11th floor brings a touch of nature to the office environment while creating a visual separation between the conference room and the private lounge.

Pegatron Shanghai Campus

Design/Completion: 2006/2009
Shanghai, China
42,000 square meters

Pegatron Corporation's Shanghai campus is situated in the suburban part of Nanhui Technology Park, where the majority of buildings have a plain, industrial appearance. The design approach for the Pegatron complex, however, was to extract elements from the style, materials and construction methods of traditional houses in southeastern China and to blend them with a touch of inspiration from the local architecture. The result is a vivid corporate image that retains regional distinctions in the time of globalization.

The office buildings are configured as a quadrangle forming an open space in the center. The entry from the plank bridge through the courtyard adds to the hierarchy of space. The exterior finish of the materials is carried into the interior space through a full-height glazed wall between the courtyard and the lobby. The water feature in the foyer embodies the Chinese idiom "water from four sides gathering in the mansion," and helps to alleviate the summer heat. The inner court in the office area adopts the square proportions of a southern Chinese residence, with a stepping rooftop that accommodates a sky garden, echoing the serene square landscape at the ground level.

The façade dimensions are modularized by 800 millimeters—a measurement slightly smaller than the common denomination of modern architecture, derived from the proportions of traditional houses to emphasize the sensitive human scale in vernacular architecture. The accent wall is made of local shed-thin tiles, and traditional building façade components are applied to the walls to achieve a distant yet familiar effect. Full-size mock-ups were constructed as a part of the bricklaying process to ensure superior artistry and interesting visual effects. The meticulous joint details of the aluminum window frames recessed in the brick walls subtly convey a contemporary sensibility.

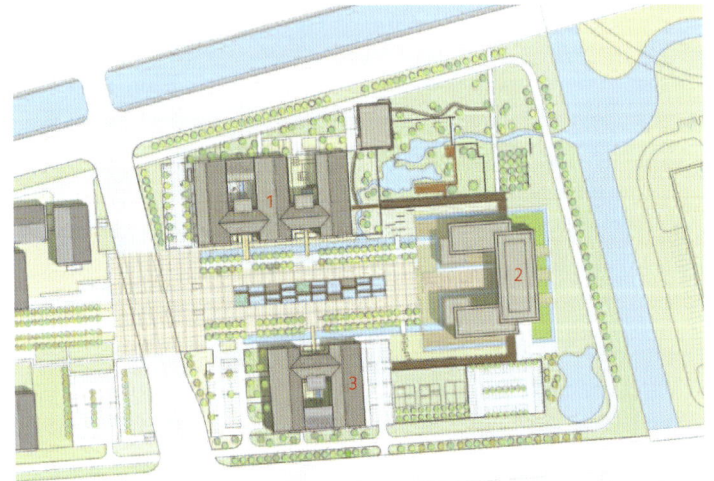

Site plan

1 Office building phase I
2 Headquarters building
3 Office building phase II

0   80m

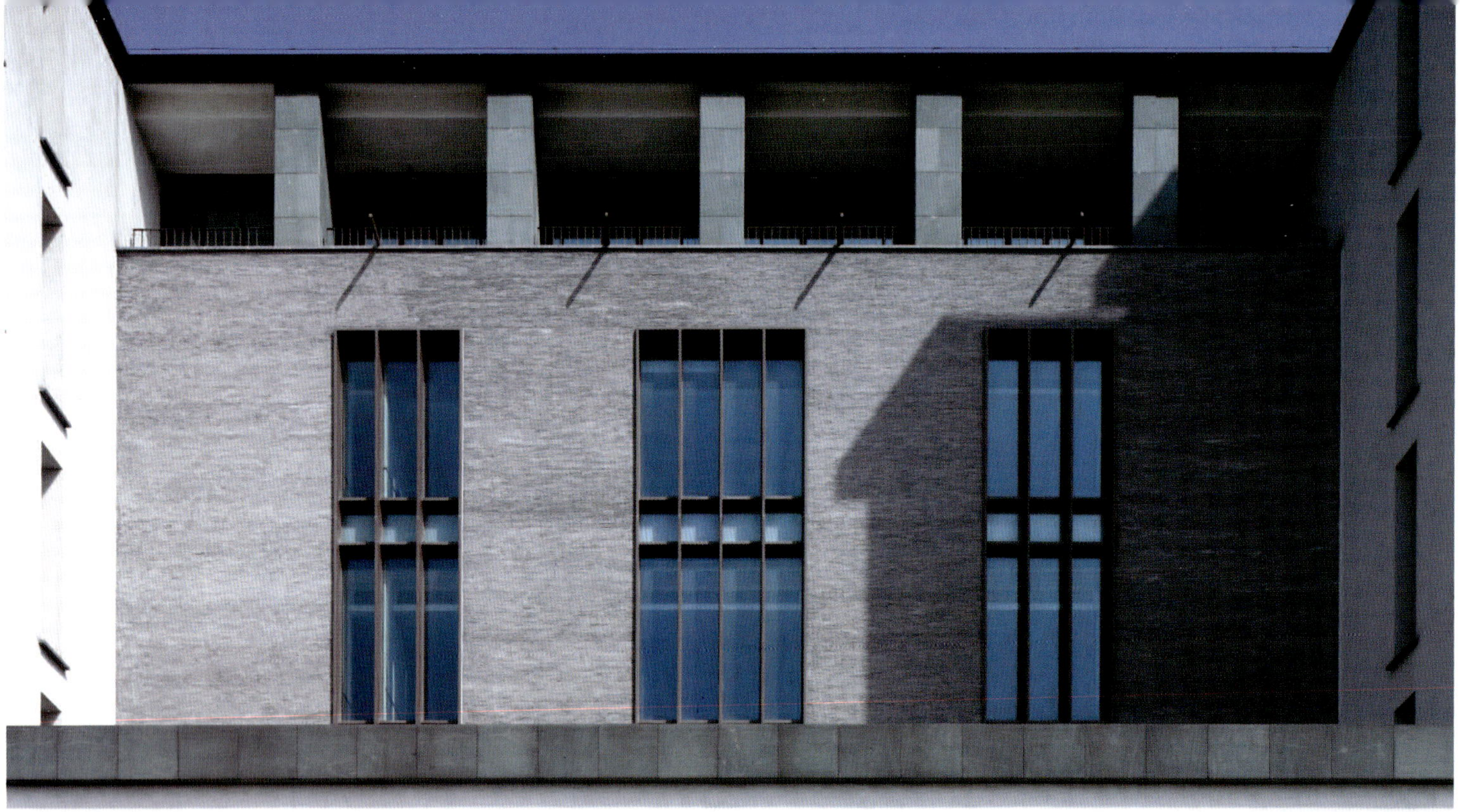

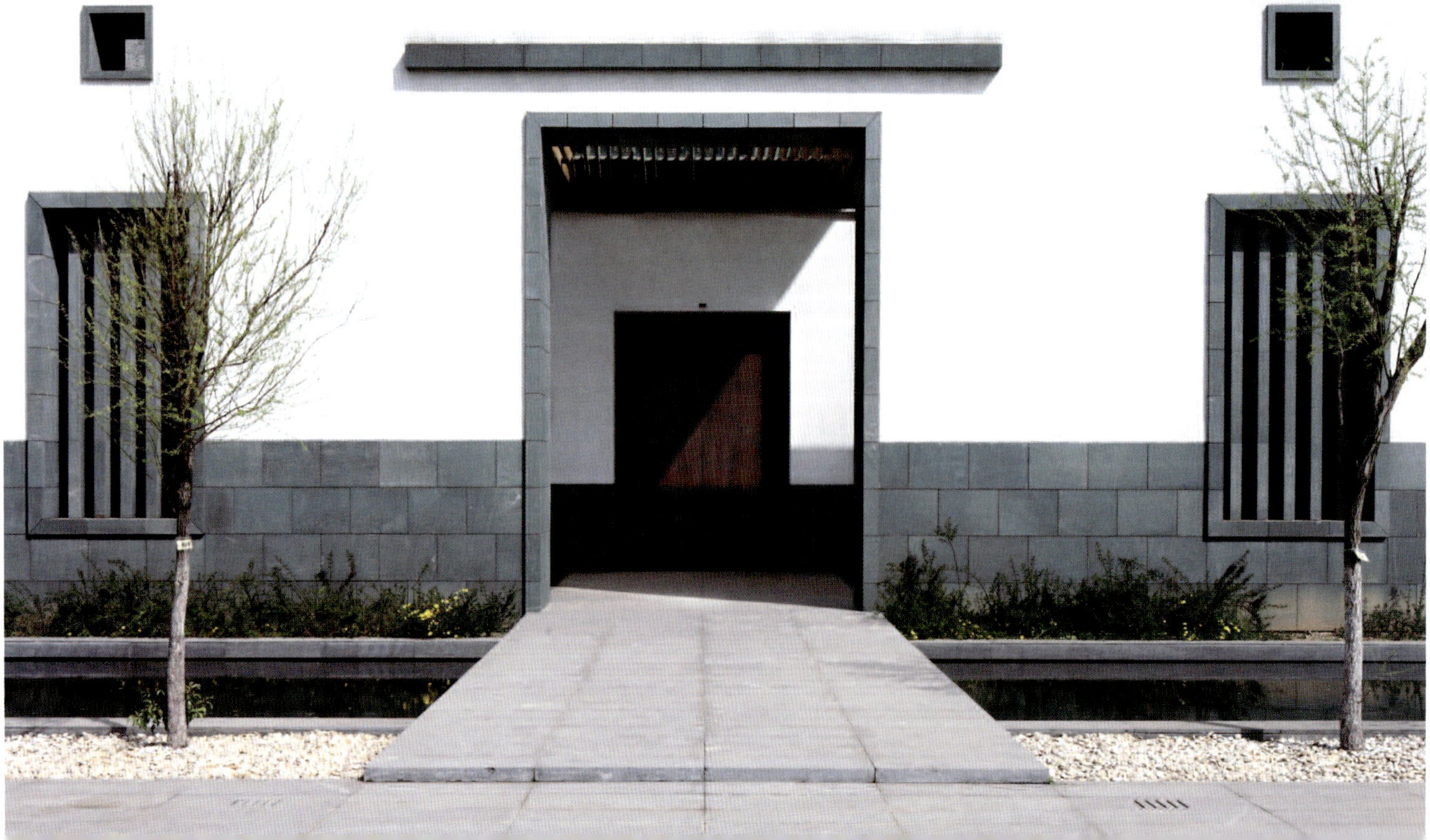

Second floor plan

1 Dormitory
2 Lounge
3 Office
4 Canteen
5 VIP dining room
6 Kitchen

Typical floor plan

1 Dormitory
2 Lounge
3 Office
4 Meeting room
5 VIP room

Sixth floor plan

1 Dormitory
2 Suite duplex
3 Lounge
4 Office
5 VIP lounge
6 Laundry
7 Meeting room

0   20m

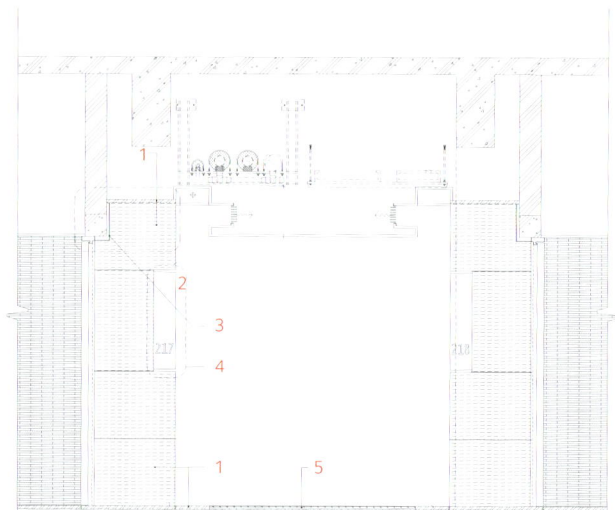

Office main lobby interior sectional elevation

1 Flame-finished stone panel
2 Removable acrylic panel
3 Metal panel cladding
4 Department signage
5 Carpet tile
6 Baked enamel steel lighting box

7 Stone sill
8 Silk laminated glass
9 Quarry tile
10 Gray brick cornice
11 Lighting fixture
12 Flame-finished stone wainscot panel

Detailed section at corridor wall

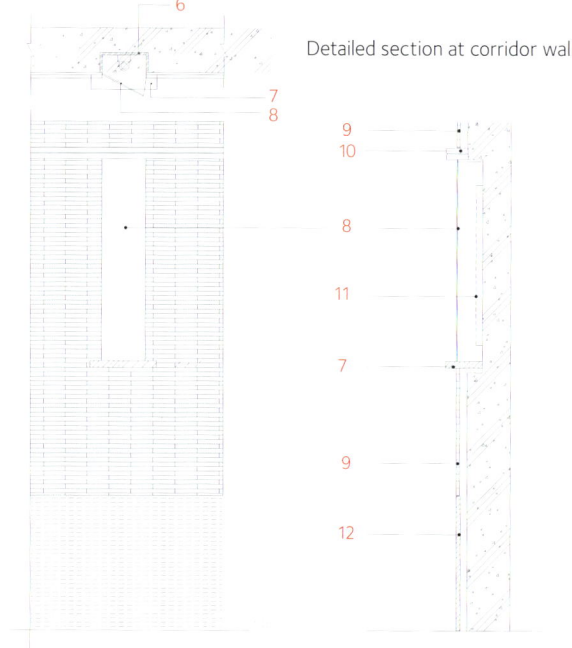

Dormitory corridor section detail

Steel frames with silk-screened tempered glass are used in the conference room partitions as a recollection of carved wooden screens. To create a floating effect that defies gravity, the transparent panels are placed at the bottom rather than the usual top configuration. As a substitute for a masonry partition, the staff canteen features a six-arched floral-patterned grill made of cast iron to achieve a unique visual effect.

In an era enraptured with ever-changing fashion, this project takes an opposite approach, pursuing quality, timeless design in place of ephemeral novelty.

Cove tile pattern screen wall assembly diagram

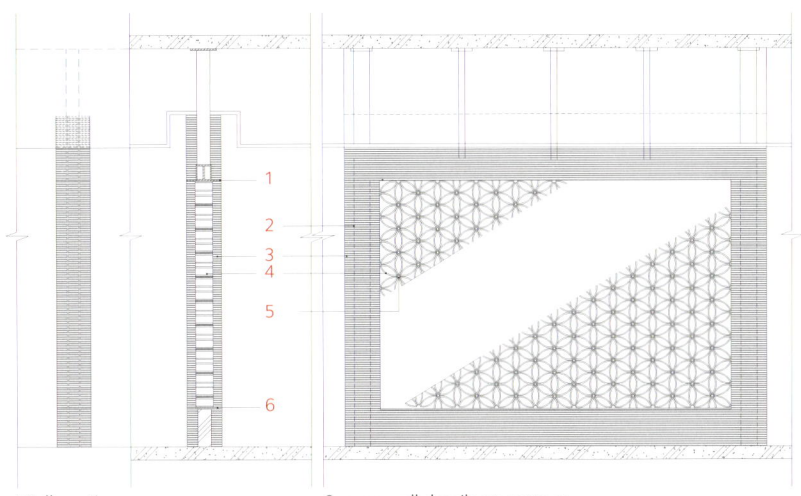

1 Baked enamel steel
   structure members
2 Enclosed steel post
3 Running course gray brick
4 Cove tiles
5 Baked enamel steel ring
6 Black stone panel

Wall section

Screen wall details at canteen

Gymnasium, Chinese Culture University

Design/Completion: 2000/2005
Taipei
54,600 square meters
Joint venture: Chiu-Hwa Wang

Situated on Yang-Ming Mountain, the new gymnasium for the Chinese Culture University, which incorporates a Chinese motif in the campus design, has expansive views of Taipei City and is surrounded by a scenic mountainous landscape. The challenge faced by J. J. Pan and Partners was the need to respond to the existing campus architecture while at the same time to create a gymnasium on a scale that did not encroach on the surroundings. The program consisted of classrooms, a gym with two levels of ball courts, and a swimming pool. Since the program already presented itself on two different scales, the decision to create two masses—an L-shaped building and an oval volume—helped reduce the overall height of the new complex.

The L-shaped wing of the complex contains the classrooms. Its volume and the geometry of its sloped roof respond to the original campus design. The oval volume, which is a response to the contours of the existing campus, houses the basketball courts and swimming pool, and is separated from the L-shaped wing by a large staircase. This void between the two volumes acts both as a physical and a spatial connector to the various campus activities. Simultaneously, it allows for a clear articulation of the forms and functions of the complex.

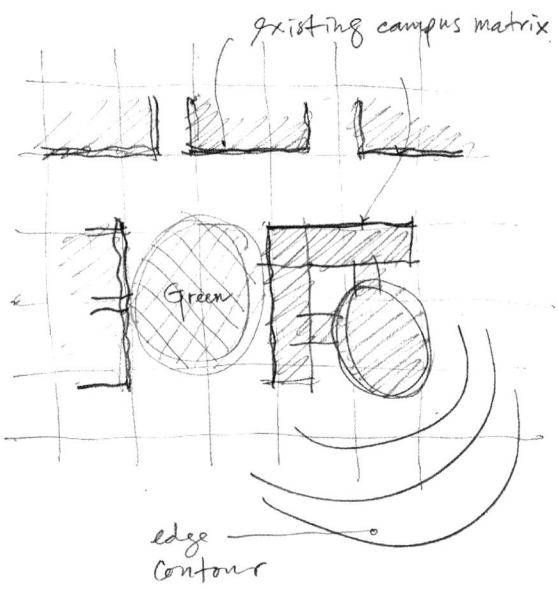

The main space of the gymnasium required maximum floor area without any vertical obstructions. Together with the engineers, the design team determined that an innovative structural arch system with four mega-piers tied together was able to provide enough support and allow the roof to cantilever out from the main structure. Each arch tapers as it is cantilevered out, and is tied back to the mega-column with floor plates. To maintain seismic stability, replaceable unbounded bracing that acts as a shock absorber was designed at specific locations. This structural innovation works not only with the building's geometry, but also allows for a cladding system that appears as a transparent skin. The contrast between the transparent oval volume and the L-shaped wing further enhances the relationship of the campus with the surrounding site.

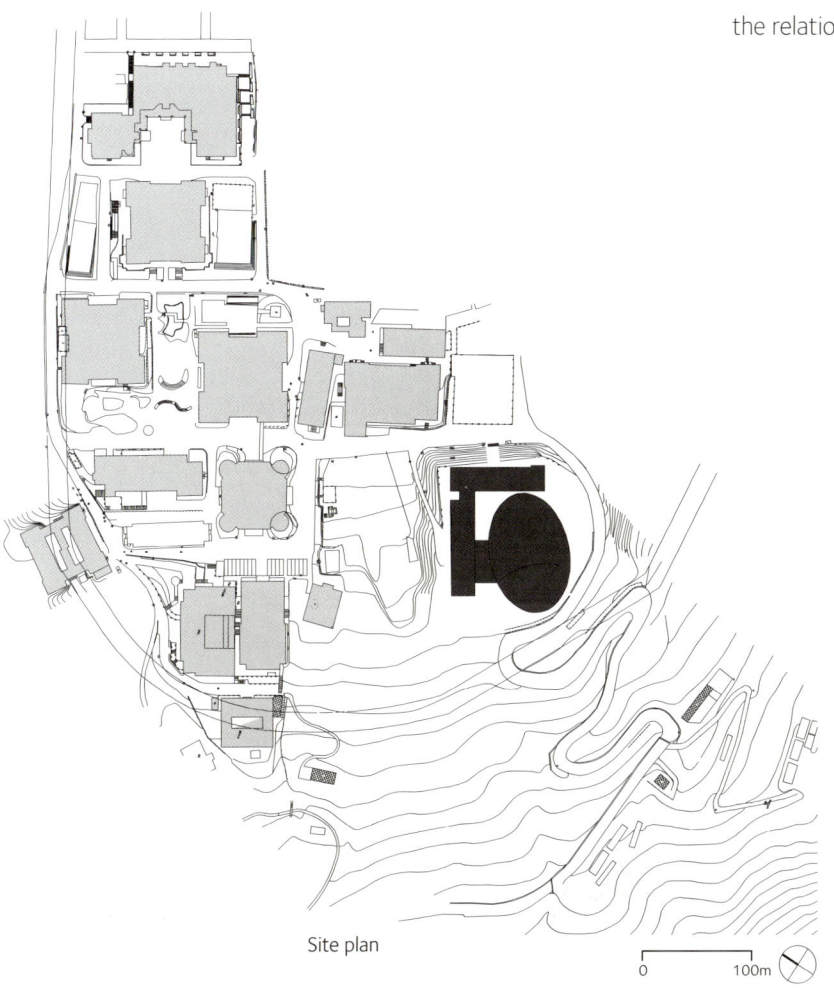

Site plan

0   100m

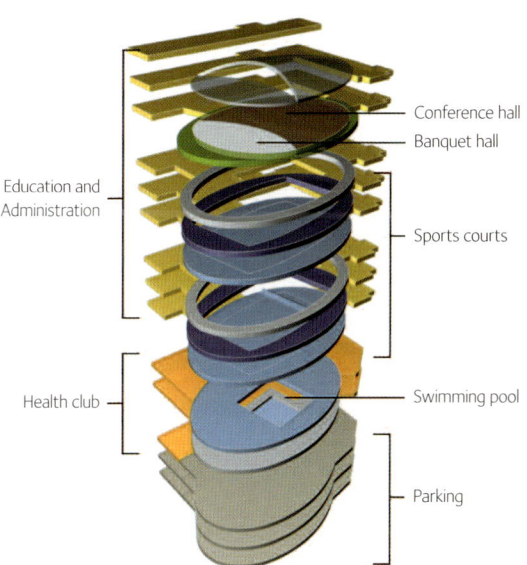

Conference hall
Banquet hall
Education and
Administration
Sports courts
Health club
Swimming pool
Parking

113

  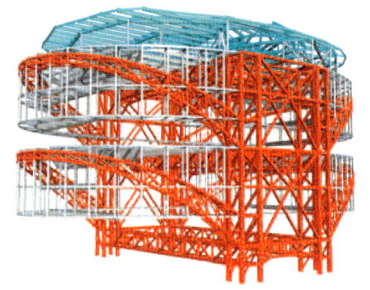

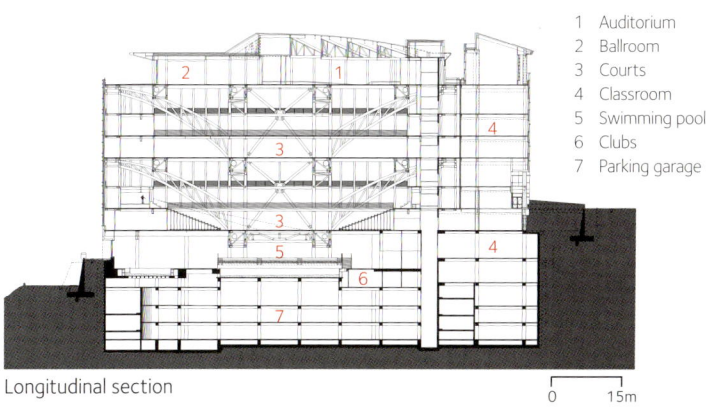

Longitudinal section

1 Auditorium
2 Ballroom
3 Courts
4 Classroom
5 Swimming pool
6 Clubs
7 Parking garage

0   15m

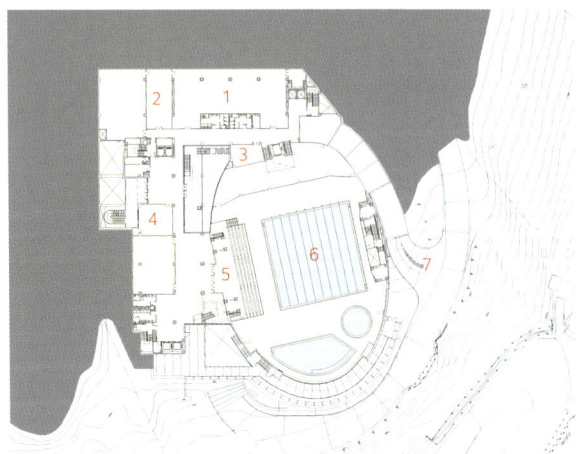

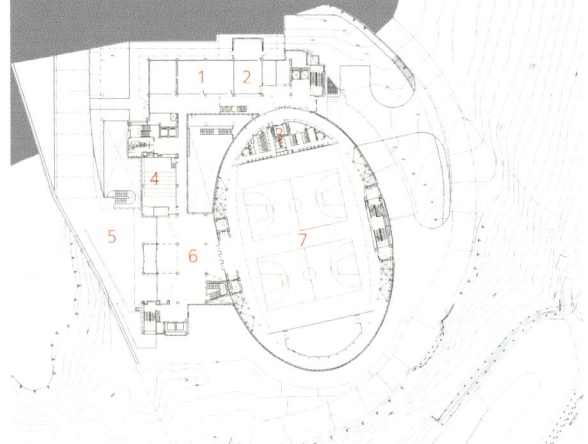

Ground floor plan

1 Training room
2 Weight training room
3 Storage
4 Massage room
5 Seating area
6 Swimming pool
7 Parking ramp

Second floor plan

1 Exhibition
2 Storage
3 Preparation room
4 Classroom
5 Plaza
6 Lobby
7 Competition court

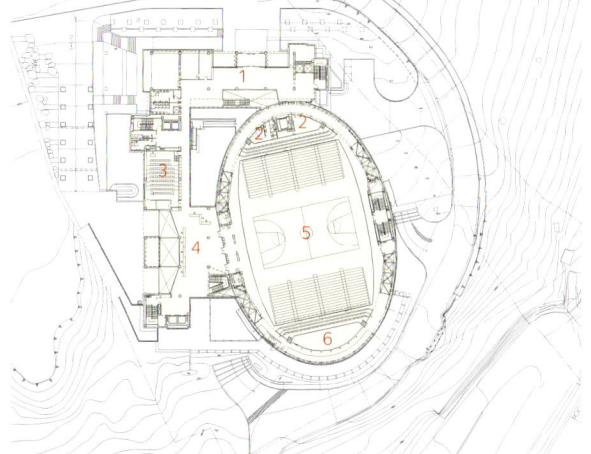

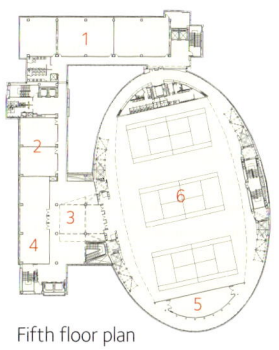

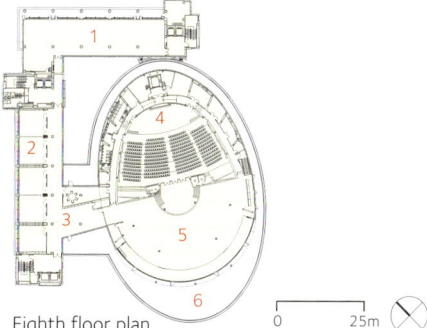

Third floor plan

1 Lobby
2 Preparation room
3 Lecture hall
4 Lobby
5 Open to court below (2F)
6 Control room

Fifth floor plan

1 Classroom
2 Administration
3 Lobby
4 Multi-function room
5 Storage
6 Practice court

Eighth floor plan

1 Vision lab
2 Conference room
3 Gallery
4 Auditorium
5 Ballroom
6 Observatory deck

0   25m

ZyXEL Recreation Center

Design/Completion: 2004/2007
Hsinchu Science Park, Taiwan
23,780 square meters

As a leader in the global communications technology industry, ZyXEL Corporation believes that innovation comes from continual stimulation by constantly changing surroundings. The aim of the recreation center is to provide employees with an environment in which they can relieve stress both physically and mentally. Throughout the facility, comfortable gathering places are strategically placed and designed to encourage interaction between staff of different departments. Since designers and research engineers can gain a technological edge through enhanced networking and dialogue, their interaction with the surrounding spaces, including personal workspace, is paramount. Since the completion of these amenities, there has been a noticeable improvement in productivity and creativity.

The building consists of three parts: the gymnasium, the activities center and the classroom. The different height and function of each separated volume are explicitly represented on the building façade as a composition of solid and transparent massing. The placement of horizontal windows for the gymnasium was determined by careful study of the sun's trajectory to ensure a sufficient level of daylight without glare and to provide unobstructed views of the meadow outside.

Structural design plays an important role in achieving the building's simple and clean configuration. The column-free gymnasium enclosure is supported by an efficient three-hinged steel truss system: the bow-shaped truss gives the long-span roof a sense of lightness, while a vertical support with similar curvature helps eliminate the need for heavy lateral bracing. Digital model simulation was utilized to ensure the best visual aspect for all structural members. Linear air supply grills on the floor work together with the roof overhang and clerestory to induce air flow through the louver to reduce cooling load.

Ground floor plan

1 Lobby
2 Gymnasium
3 Table tennis room
4 Café
5 Loading dock
6 Parking ramp

0   20m

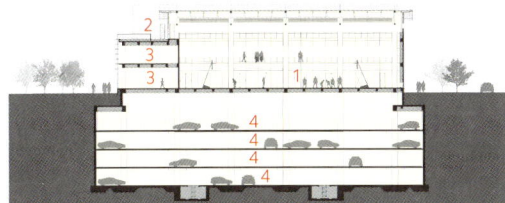

Transverse section

1 Gymnasium
2 Roof patio
3 Café
4 Parking garage

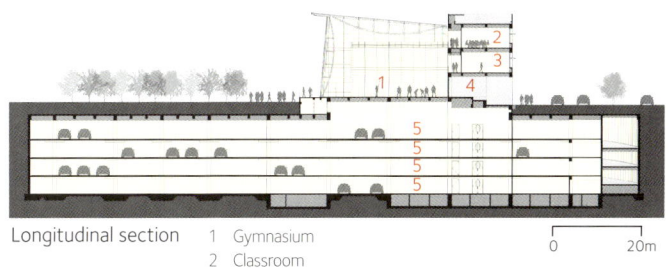

Longitudinal section

1 Gymnasium
2 Classroom
3 Fitness center
4 Loading dock
5 Parking garage

0   20m

Located in a designated park, the building occupies less than 15 per cent of the site, in order to preserve as much green space as possible. The permeable pavement and multiple layers of shrubs are arranged in simple geometry to match the building's modern façade in the background. Four levels of extended underground parking is provided to help relieve the parking needs of the public and the company's employees working in the main building across the street.

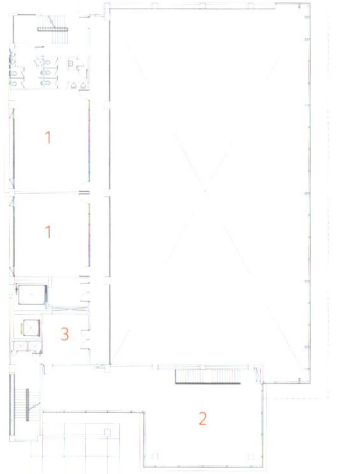

1 Fitness center
2 Café
3 Elevator lobby

Second floor plan

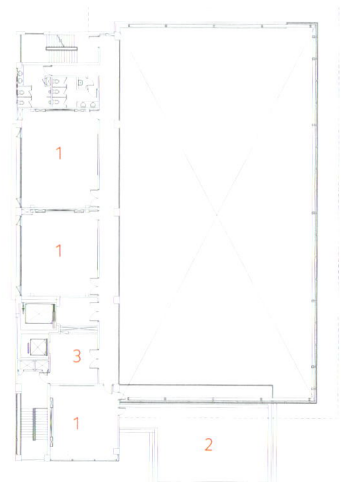

1 Classroom
2 Roof patio
3 Elevator lobby

Third floor plan

0   10m

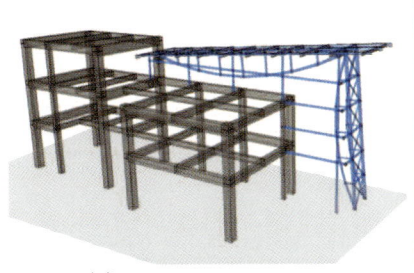

Structural diagram

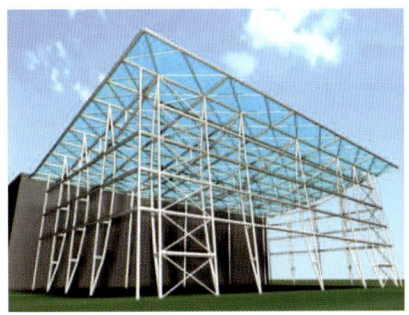

Fleur de Chine Hotel, Sun Moon Lake

Design/Completion: 2001/2007
Nanto, Taiwan
27,600 square meters

With its rich cultural background and abundance of lush natural resources, Sun Moon Lake has long been one of Taiwan's most popular tourist destinations, attracting annually, millions of visitors. At dawn and dusk, mist gathers over the surface of the water, creating a scene of mesmerizing beauty. Located at the tip of a peninsula on the north shore, the Fleur de Chine Hotel enjoys breathtaking panoramic views of the lake and natural surrounds.

Rebuilt on the historical site of the original hotel, which was destroyed by the earthquake of 1999, the reborn hotel establishes Fleur de Chine with a new brand identity and a refreshed image. The lower portion of the building is partially embedded into the slope and merged with the surroundings to gently negotiate the 20-meter grade change. The L-shaped layout maximizes the use of windows and vistas, offering a variety of perspectives of the lake from the guestrooms. The top floor is set back to create a lightweight skyline that echoes the layering of the mountain range. Materials that complement the textures and subdued tones of the surroundings give the building a sense of simplicity, harmonizing with the beauty of the lake's natural environment.

In consideration of sustainability, the landscape design restores the living systems of the site by reintroducing indigenous plants as well as a series of ecological ponds that emulate the original contour lines of the hill. The use of dimmed lights in the garden not only minimizes light pollution but also adds to the shimmering nighttime wonder at the lakeshore.

1 Entry plaza
2 Parking entrance
3 Main building
4 Terrace
5 Water lily pond
6 Viewing platform
7 Outdoor theater
8 Lawn
9 Tanning platform

Site plan

0   30m

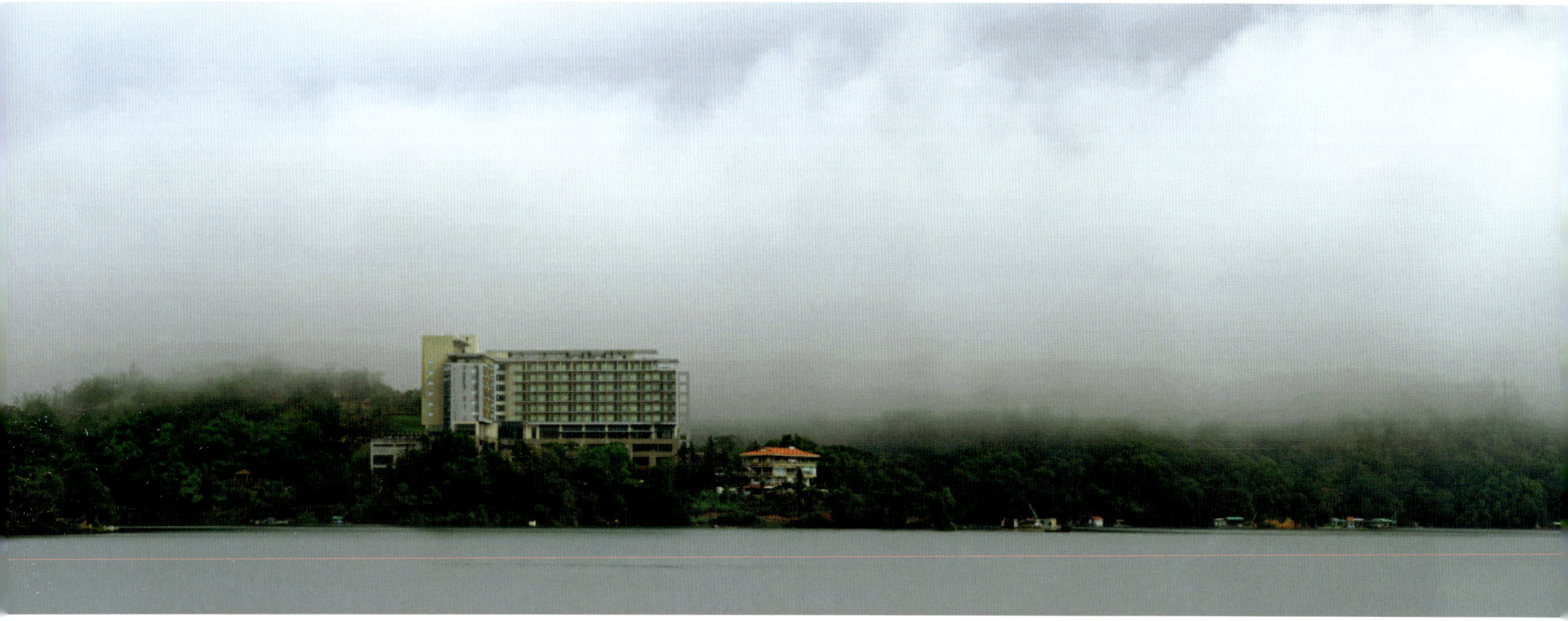

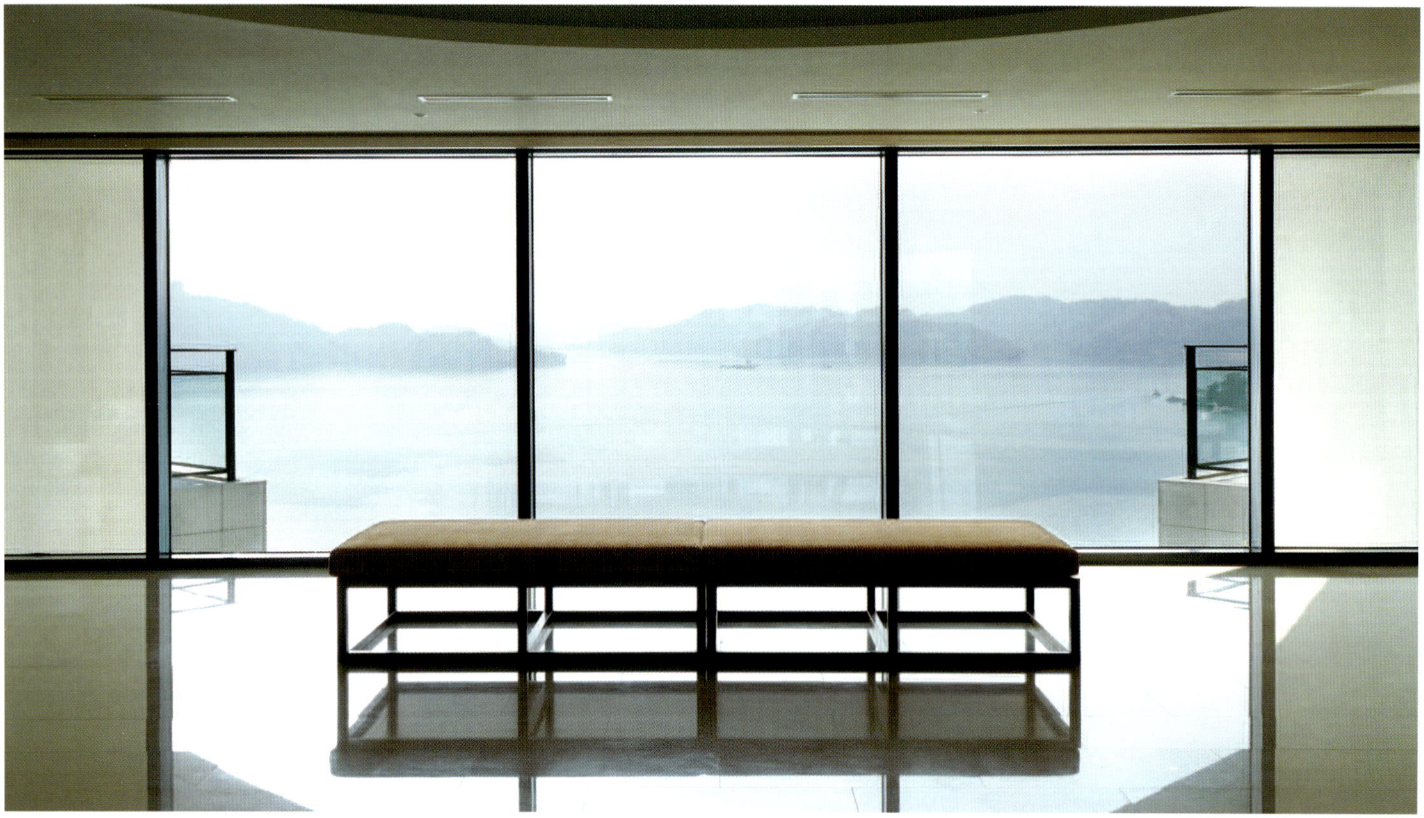

Of the greatest cultural significance to the Sun Moon Lake area is the history of the Shao Tribes, who lived by the water's edge for thousands of years. Their heritage is recognized in the hotel's architecture through the use of traditional colors, textures and patterns. The entry plaza of the hotel features mosaic paving with figures from tribal mythology, including deer, owls and javanica trees. The local folk art and artifacts integrated in the design of the hotel enrich the architectural journey by showcasing Taiwan's rich aboriginal culture to international visitors.

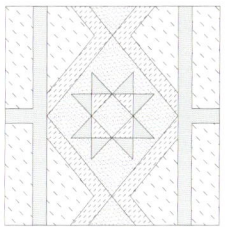

 Pink granite

 Gray granite

 Beige granite

 Light gray granite

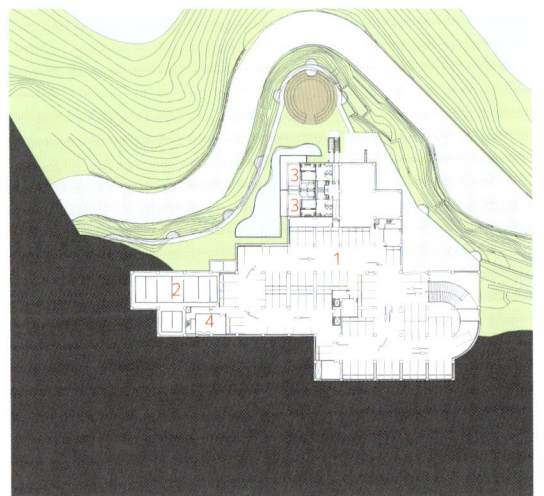

Basement floor plan

1　Parking garage
2　Water tank
3　Spa
4　Mechanical room

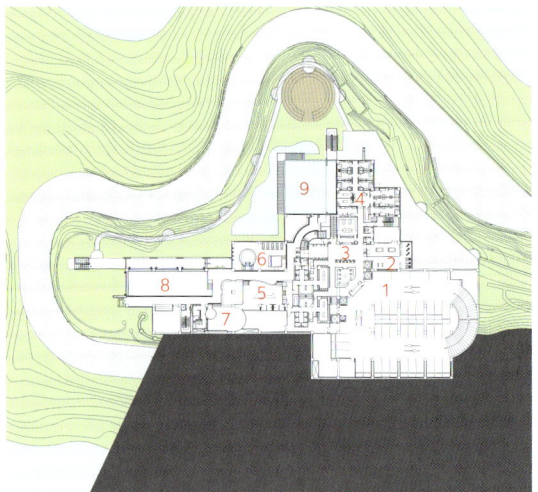

Ground floor plan

1　Parking garage
2　Fitness center
3　Hot spring lobby
4　Indoor spa
5　Kurhaus
6　Massage center
7　Children's pool
8　Swimming pool
9　Water lily pond

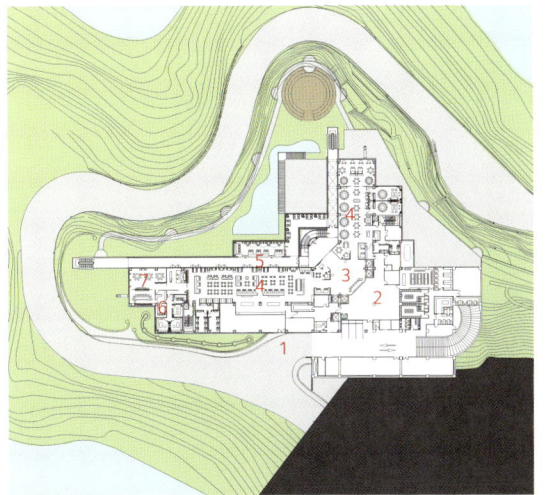

First floor plan

1 Parking entrance
2 Kitchen
3 Lobby
4 Restaurant
5 Terrace / outdoor dining
6 Private KTV lounge
7 Teppanyaki restaurant

Second floor plan

1 Entry plaza
2 Lobby
3 Group entry
4 Lounge bar
5 Ballroom / conference
6 Meeting room
7 Children's playground
8 Tea salon

0   30m

Section

1 Lobby
2 Guestrooms
3 Lounge bar
4 Hot spring lobby
5 Kitchen
6 Parking garage

A cantilevered frame over the setback at the top floor completes the overall building massing and provides shading for the terrace.

Neo Solar Power Office Building Complex

Design/Completion: 2007/2009
Hsinchu Science Park, Taiwan
47,940 square meters

Neo Solar Power's building complex is located in a newly reclaimed zone in Hsinchu Science Park (HSP). The project site, facing a major access road from the park's main boulevard and bordering an 80-meter-wide greenbelt, is regarded as one of the most prominent land parcels in the area. It is the owner's expectation that the new building will become a dramatic architectural landmark among the Science Park's high-tech companies.

Emphasizing the link between NSP's corporate identity and its advanced photovoltaic production technology became the most challenging design task. The photoelectric effect, which is the basis of solar energy engineering, is abstracted in architectural form by transforming the sine-curved light wave into a faceted glass curtain wall. The result is a clean yet striking façade rhythmically undulating against the sun and playfully reflecting the green meadow in the foreground.

The structure consists of two sections: an eight-story research and development (R & D) facility with an auditorium, a staff canteen, laboratories and offices to the north and a five-level manufacturing plant to the south. The manufacturing complex's solid massing of aluminum panels contrasts the transparency of the office building's semi-reflective glass curtain wall façade. The circulation aisle along the perimeter of each floor faces the exterior greenbelt, and provides staff with space for constructive meetings and discussions. A full-height glazed wall on the north east maximizes the vista of the vast greenbelt surrounding the R & D compound.

The zigzag configuration of floor slabs holding the wall panels in place follows the shape of the building. Eight distinct specifications of trapezoid units, each with 350 different sized glass panes, were designed to achieve the complex 49.5 degrees inclining and 96.7 degrees sloping angles, optimizing construction and maintenance of the complex curtain wall.

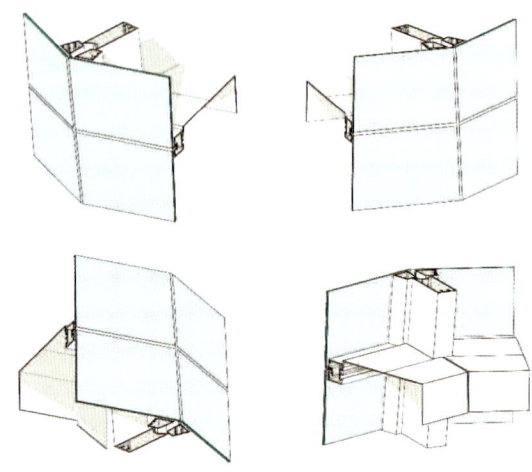

Glass curtain wall details

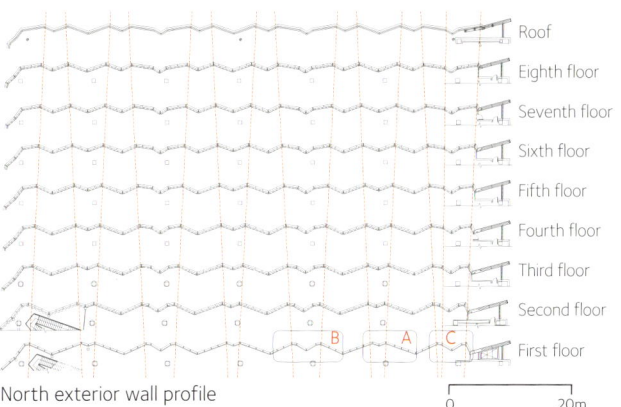

Roof
Eighth floor
Seventh floor
Sixth floor
Fifth floor
Fourth floor
Third floor
Second floor
First floor

North exterior wall profile

0   20m

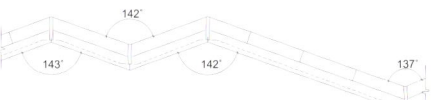

142°
143°   142°   137°

Floor plate peripheral profile type A

120°
147°   159°   159°   147°

Floor plate peripheral profile type B

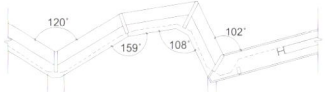

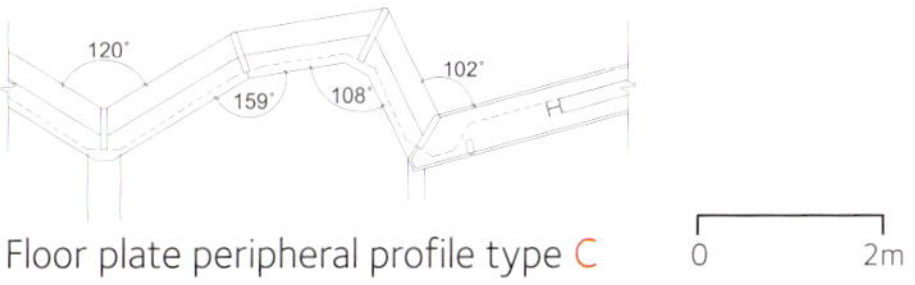

120°
159°   108°   102°

Floor plate peripheral profile type C

0   2m

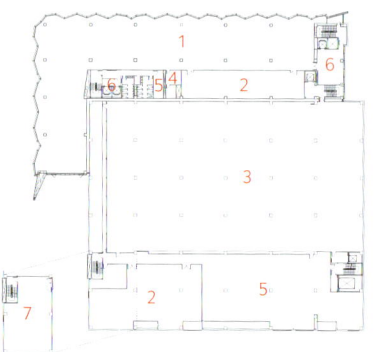

1 Office area
2 Storage
3 Production area
4 Kitchenette
5 Mechanical room
6 Elevator lobby
7 Mezzanine

Typical floor plan

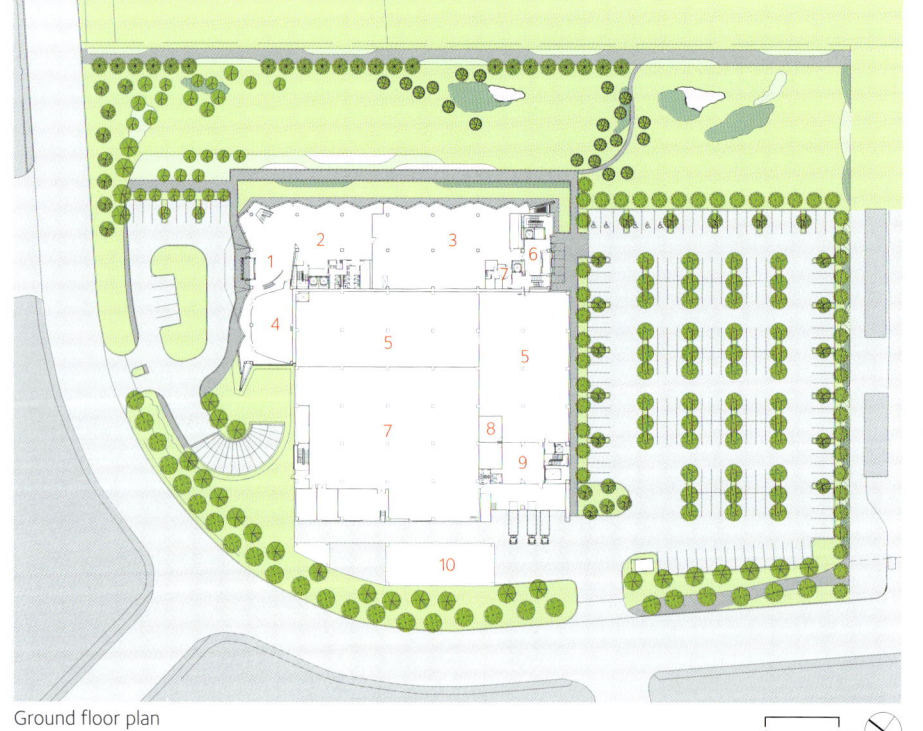

1 Lobby
2 Conference room
3 Canteen
4 Auditorium
5 Warehouse
6 Elevator lobby
7 Mechanical room
8 Office
9 Sorting area
10 Storage

Ground floor plan

0   20m

Huga Fab III and Headquarters Building

Design/Completion: 2007/2009
Central Taiwan Science Park, Taiwan
31,860 square meters

As a signature landmark located near the entrance to the Science Park, the simplistic beauty of the Huga Headquarters building sets an example for what is possible in the design of industrial buildings. The two major building volumes are configured as an abstraction of the LED manufacturing process, resembling the electric discharge between electrodes.

The loading zone and parking entrance are located at the lowest point of the parcel near the southeast corner of the site in order to take advantage of the 6-meter grade differential. Fabrication buildings are set back and away from the northeast border, creating a generous entrance.

The ground level, with a 9-meter floor-to-floor height, is used for manufacturing LED epitaxial wafer and crystalline grain. The LED strip lighting element features the "HUGA" corporate logo on the northern façade. The six-level office building orients north-to-south; its insulated aluminum wall panels and glass curtain wall achieve excellent energy performance while maximizing the view overlooking the scenic Dadu Mountains nearby.

The composition of the building's four elevations features deep setback windows and sunshades. Vertical and horizontal grills are carefully studied for the proper position of frames, columns, joints and alignment to express the rational and meticulous professionalism of the corporation.

1 Executive office
2 Office area
3 Conference room
4 VIP guest room
5 Mechanical room
6 Elevator lobby

Sixth floor plan

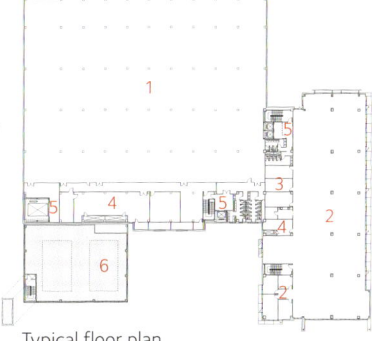

1 Production area
2 Office area
3 Conference room
4 Mechanical room
5 Elevator lobby
6 Roof mechanical room

Typical floor plan

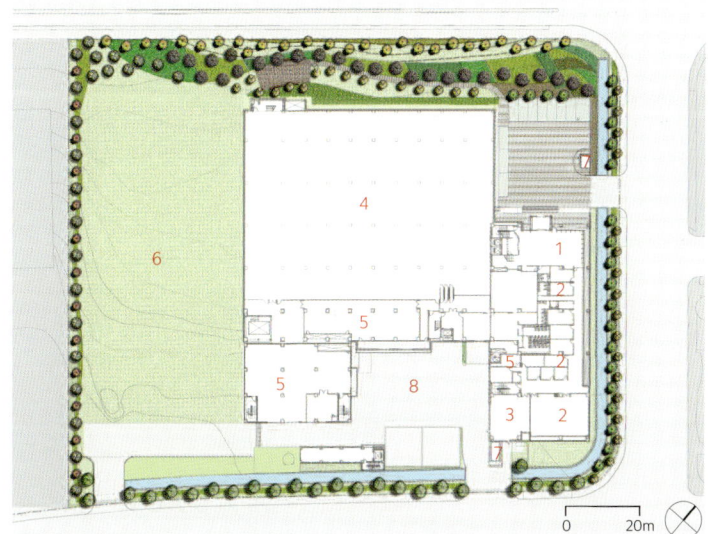

Ground floor plan

1 Lobby
2 Conference room
3 Office
4 Production area

5 Mechanical room
6 Expansion space for 2nd phase
7 Security office
8 Service area at B1

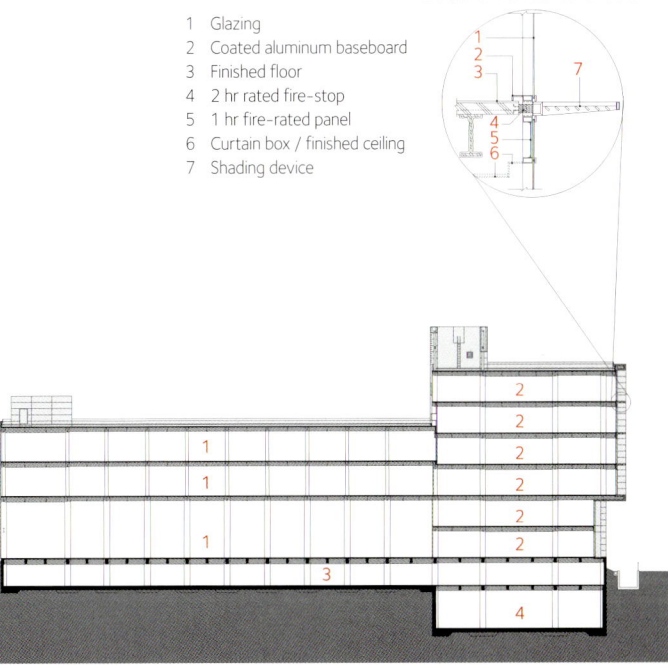

Detail of horizontal shade

1 Glazing
2 Coated aluminum baseboard
3 Finished floor
4 2 hr rated fire-stop
5 1 hr fire-rated panel
6 Curtain box / finished ceiling
7 Shading device

Longitudinal section

1 Production area
2 Office area
3 Parking
4 Water treatment tank

0   20m

IMPAX Lab Taiwan Plant Phase I

Design/Completion: 2007/2009
Chunan Science Park, Taiwan
12,724 square meters

In the pharmaceutical industry, the color white symbolizes cleanness and purity. It is also precisely the image the United States firm, IMPAX, aimed to project through its first facility in Taiwan.

The 12-meter-high jointless exterior wall encloses the main functions of laboratories and offices, creating an image of precision wrapping through its folded slabs. Though having separate functional spaces, both the laboratory and office are contained within the wraps. The programs are distinctly visible through the floor-to-ceiling window walls. The theme of duality, Impax's core concept in medicine production, is expressed through the juxtaposition of solid massing with void volume. Additionally, one of the client's advanced patents, involving stacking of micro-medicine films, is represented by the hierarchical layering of programmatic spaces. On another level, the building's vocabulary of architectural metaphors is similar to a time-release tablet that takes effect over time.

To highlight the gradual-release concept, the design utilizes blue stripe from Impax's corporate logo in random sizes, creating a vibrant pattern on the façade and setting the tone for future expansion. The curving wood strip wall in the main lobby also carries the "wrapping" theme by continuing the texture throughout the interior. The wood grains offer a warm touch to soften the sleek and modern exterior.

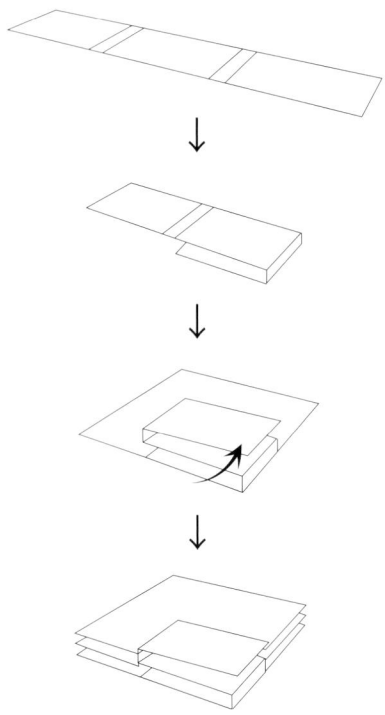

Concept—wrapping medicine with paper

1 Office
2 Mechanical room
3 Laboratory

Second floor plan

Phase 2 (in planning) ← | → Phase 1

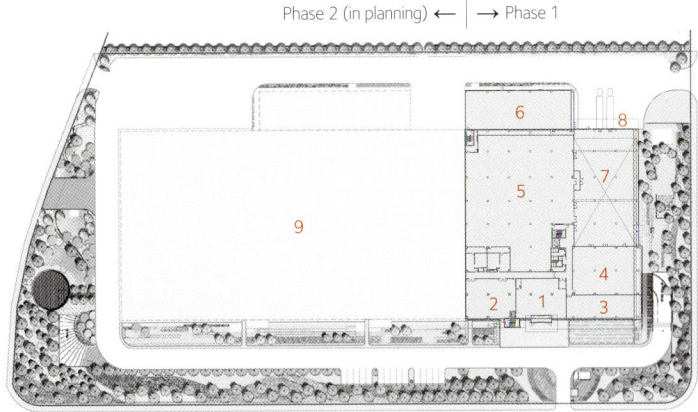

Ground floor plan

1	Lobby	6	Mechanical room
2	Canteen	7	Warehouse
3	Office area	8	Loading dock
4	Pilot production area	9	Future expansion
5	Production area		

0   30m

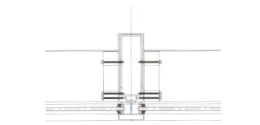

Curtain wall vertical mullion detail (A)

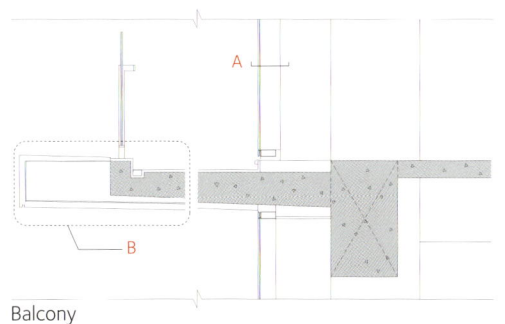

Balcony

1 Steel stud framing
2 S. S. screws
3 Drip reveal
4 Canopy composite coating
5 Facial tile
6 S. S. trench cover

7 S. S. trim
8 1:2 waterproof cement mortar
9 Floor tile

Detail of balcony (B)

0   25cm

Discourse

Church of Suang-Lien Center for the Elderly

Design/Completion: 2005/2009
Taipei
1,264 square meters

The church is located near a scenic highway on the northern coast of Taiwan. Backed by the mountains and fronting the sea, the site is endowed with a pleasant view of its natural surroundings.

The Christian symbol of "  " (representing a fish, ΙΧΘΥΣ in Greek) inspired the design of the church. Two curved lines shape the fish-like plane along the winding contour of the ditch and land boundary. The concept outlined in Isaiah 54:2-3 ("Enlarge the place of thy tent, and let them stretch forth the curtains of thine habitations") was applied in designing a complete stress-resistant structural form. Three-dimensional parameters were employed to precisely control variations of the arched planes.

The structure of the arched planes is composed of curved steel tubes 40 centimeters in diameter, with H beams forming a fish-shaped dome on top. The dome is tightly bound by a lightweight shuttle-shaped structure to create pointed arch windows on both sides.

The shell in turn is clad with aluminum sheets. A cross is carved out at the highest point to be visible along the seaside, representing Christ's love in heaven and on earth. The curved surface rises along the shoreline, blocking the sea wind.

The tent-shaped aluminum sheets, visually detached from the ground by a glass enclosed first floor that opens up to admit the beautiful scenery of the park.

Enlarge the place of thy tent, and let them stretch forth the curtains of thine habitations
– Isaiah 54:2–3

The exposed, asterisk-shaped steel grids extend to the interior and form the structural frame. The triangular space in the frame is fitted with sound-absorbing panels that allow even sound resonance. The 3-centimeter reveals between the triangular panels and the steel members not only eliminate excessive low-frequency sounds, but also highlight the structural components. Hanging curved triangular reflection panels provide the acoustic conditions required for choir recital and speech amplification. The design of the furniture takes the needs of the elderly congregation into consideration.

Site plan

1 Phase I
2 Phase II
3 Phase III

0   20m

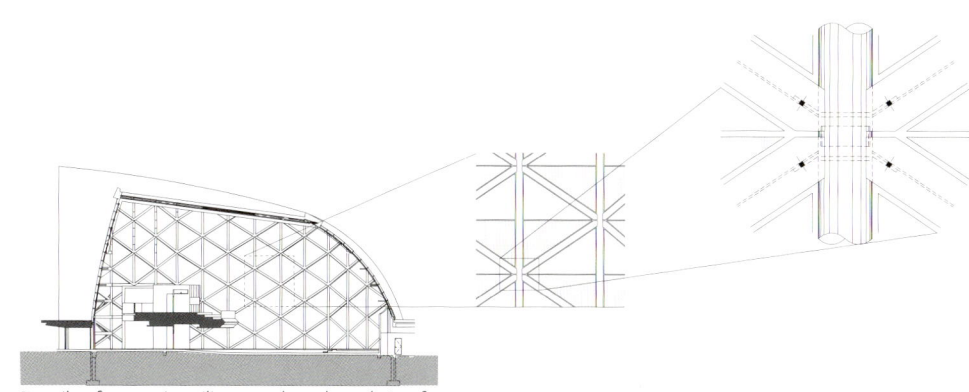

Details of acoustic ceiling panels and steel pipe frames

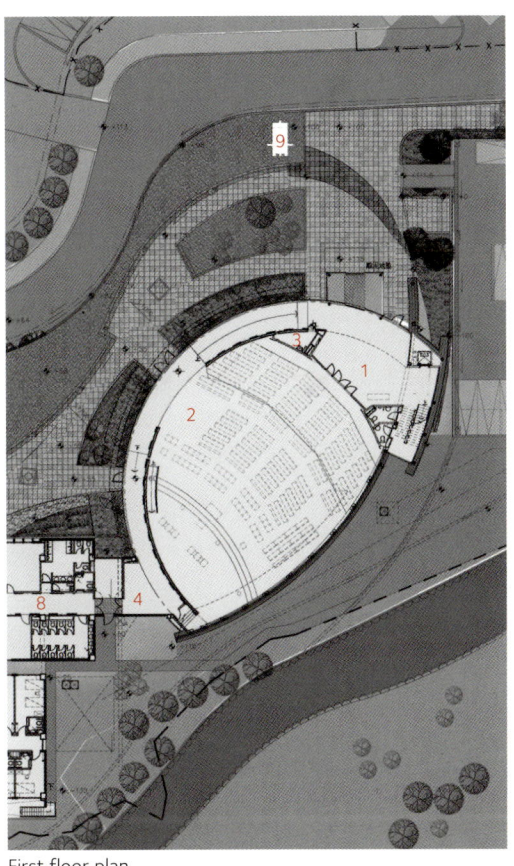

First floor plan

1 Hall
2 Sanctuary
3 Sound control room
4 Passageway
5 Foyer
6 Control room
7 Parent / child room
8 Care building
9 Bell tower

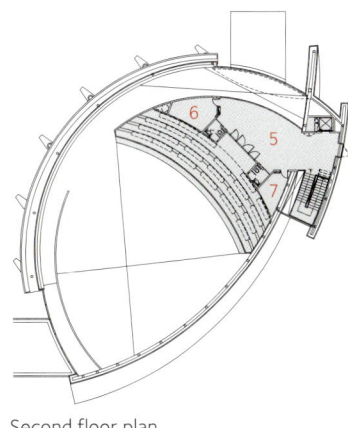

Second floor plan

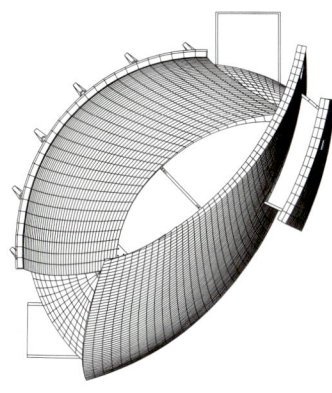

Roof plan

0   10m

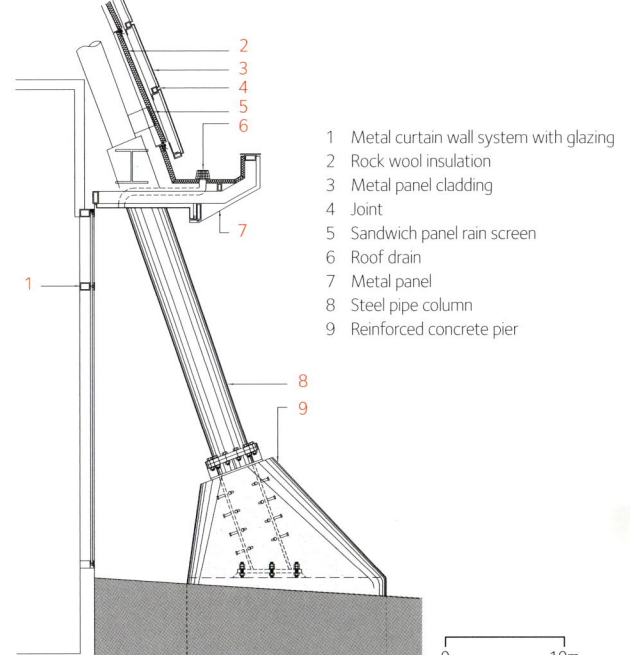

1 Metal curtain wall system with glazing
2 Rock wool insulation
3 Metal panel cladding
4 Joint
5 Sandwich panel rain screen
6 Roof drain
7 Metal panel
8 Steel pipe column
9 Reinforced concrete pier

0   10m

Section detail of steel pipe column foundation

The steel columns are stationed by wedge-shaped buttresses, clearly revealing the details of the column caps, connecting plates and articulated details.

By the entrance, the minimalist-style bell tower employs straight lines that turn upwards, overlapping in a cross shape. At night, the light cast on the curved church walls projects the image of a tent between heaven and earth, with the spiritual symbol of the cross on top. It is hoped the church will become a warm and soothing haven that gently comforts the hearts of the elderly who visit.

Taoyuan International Airport Access MRT Stations

Design/Completion: 2006/2013
Taipei
Five MRT Stations

To travelers, a rapid transit station linking the airport to a city is a place where the beginning or the end of a journey is celebrated. In its design of a series of individualistic yet iconic airport transit stations, J. J. Pan and Partners has sought to project the image of a "fast train flashing by, soaring up on silver wings."

The A2 station is built high above a dike, making it the first elevated station after the train emerges from the underground tunnel. The station platform, featuring a tube-shaped lattice structure clad in zinc-aluminum alloyed sheets, symbolizes the interwoven flow of passengers. The curved roof has a thin metal skin that lifts slightly at an angle off the horizon to give the impression of a plane taking off.

Each station along the elevated transit line is distinctively recognizable by the form and layout shaped by the surrounding urban context. Adopting the A2 station as a prototype, the A3 station inherits and duplicates its predecessor's tube-shaped roof and transforms it into an image of an aircraft hangar.

For the next three stations—A4, A5 and A6—a more modern, minimalist aesthetic further simplifies the prototype. The roof of flat metal panels is shaped to resemble folded paper planes, echoing jet planes that soar through the skies above. The fenestration of the station's buildings follows the circulation of passengers, indicating the various directions of travel. The transparent walls and windows that are features of each station act as visual links between travelers and the streetscape, helping promote the individual identity of each station's surrounding neighborhood. As trains pass by, these stations will act as portals that the diversity of urban life and the vigorous energy of the metropolis can be glimpsed through.

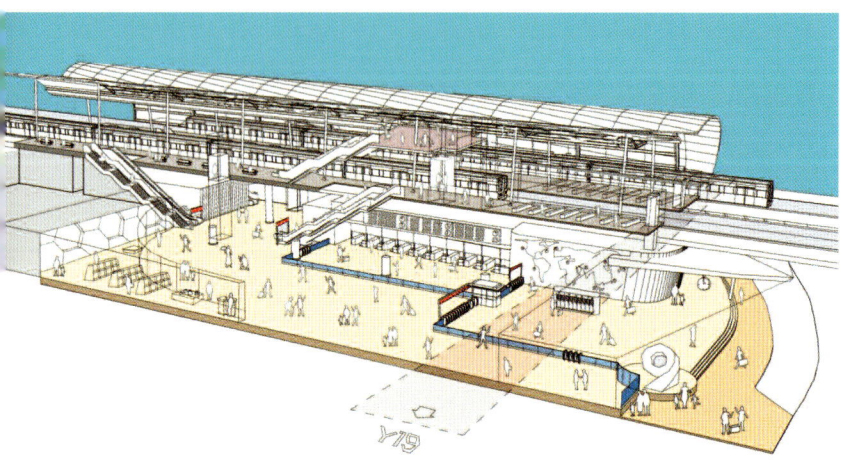

A3 station section perspective

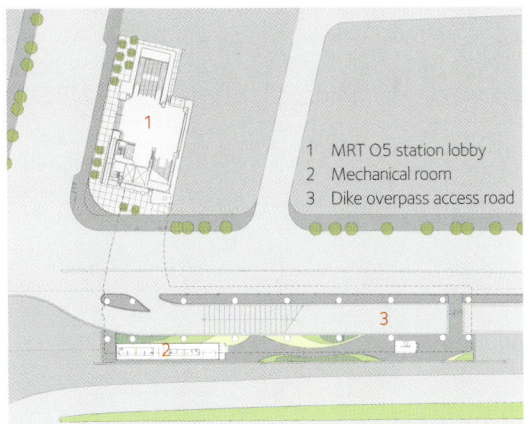

1	MRT O5 station lobby
2	Mechanical room
3	Dike overpass access road

A2 station ground level plan

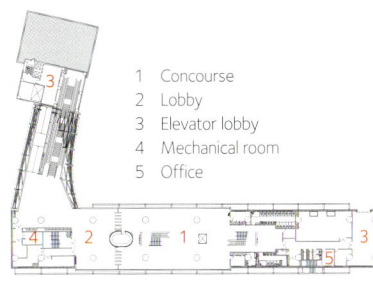

1	Concourse
2	Lobby
3	Elevator lobby
4	Mechanical room
5	Office

A2 station concourse level plan

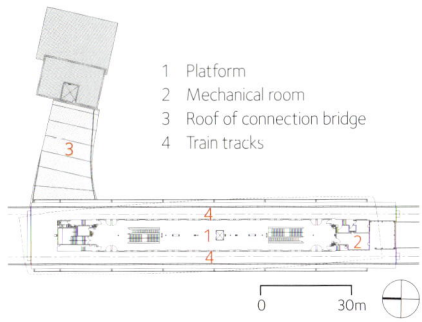

1	Platform
2	Mechanical room
3	Roof of connection bridge
4	Train tracks

0   30m

A2 station platform level plan

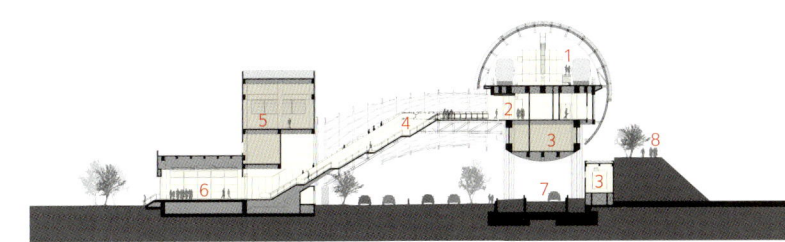

A2 station transverse section

1	Platform	5	Elevator lobby
2	Concourse	6	MRT O5 station lobby
3	Mechanical room	7	Dike overpass access road
4	Connection bridge	8	Dike overpass

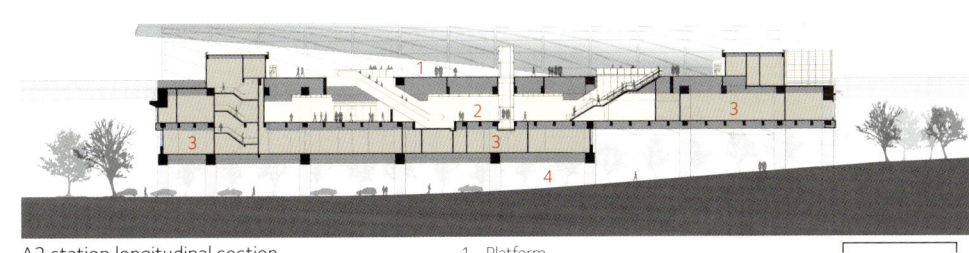

A2 station longitudinal section

1	Platform
2	Concourse level
3	Mechanical room
4	Dike overpass access road

0   20m

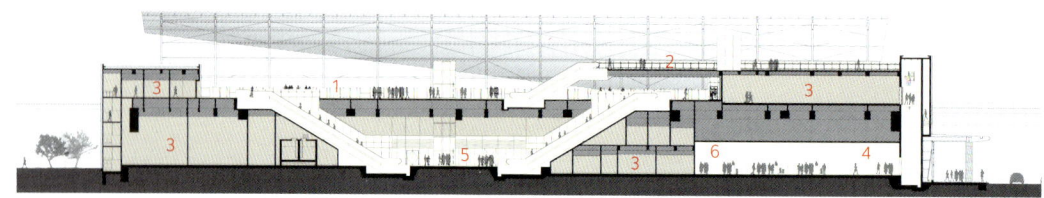

A3 station longitudlinal section

1 Platform
2 Concourse (transfer to MRT Y19 station)
3 Mechanical room
4 Baggage handling area
5 Concourse
6 In-town check-in counter

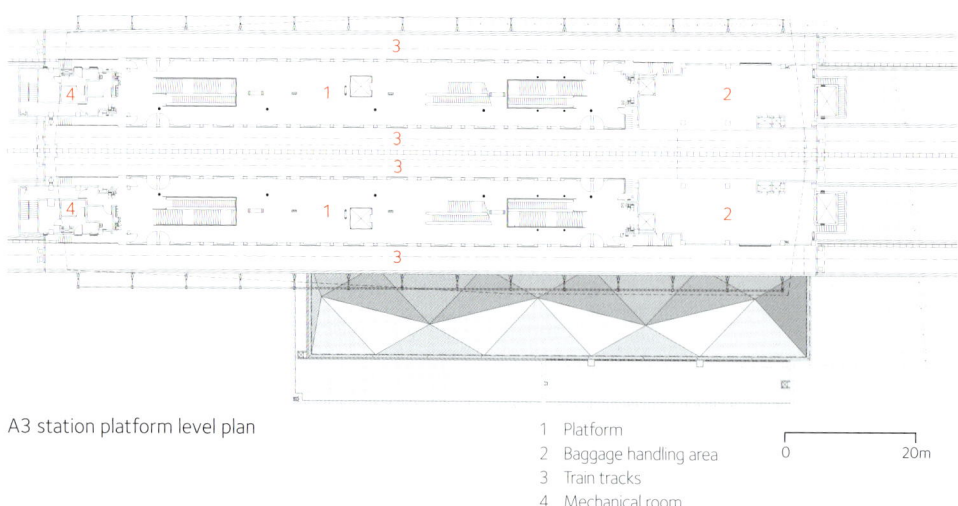

A3 station platform level plan

1 Platform
2 Baggage handling area
3 Train tracks
4 Mechanical room

0   20m

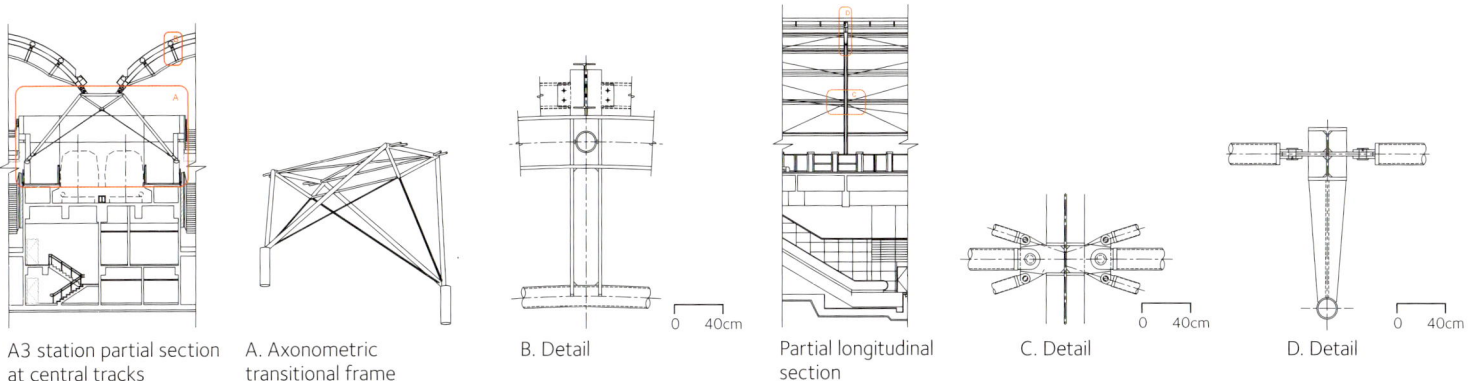

A3 station partial section at central tracks

A. Axonometric transitional frame

B. Detail

0 40cm

Partial longitudinal section

C. Detail

0 40cm

D. Detail

0 40cm

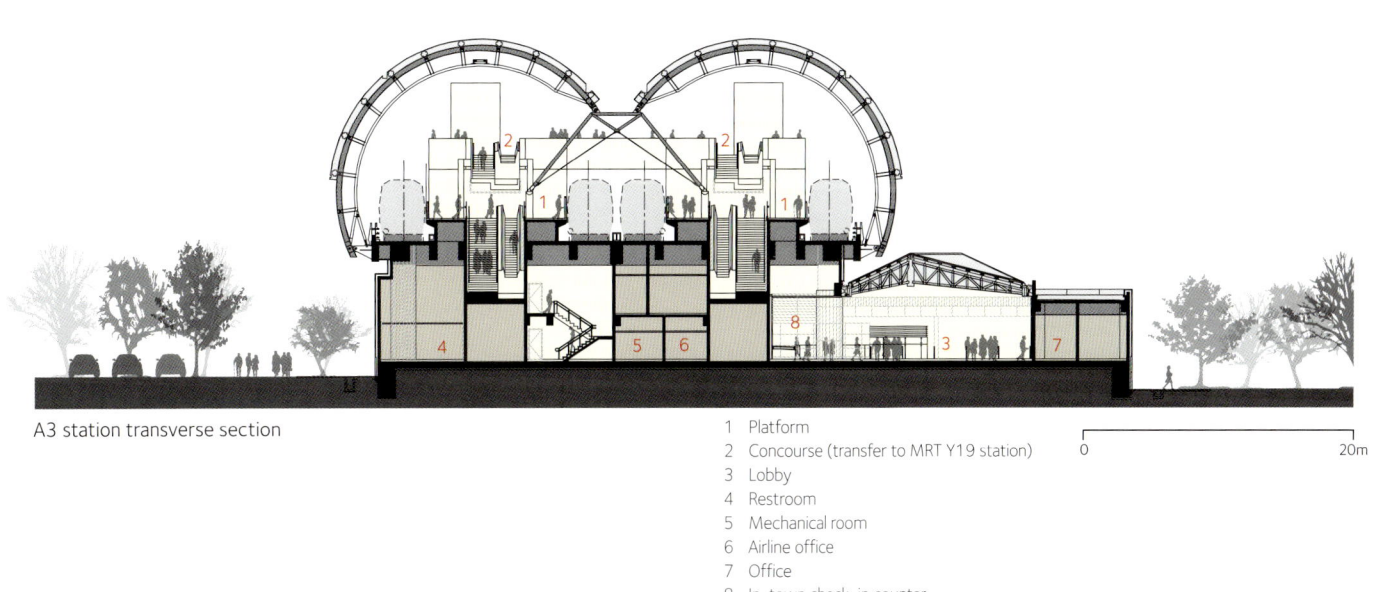

A3 station transverse section

1 Platform
2 Concourse (transfer to MRT Y19 station)
3 Lobby
4 Restroom
5 Mechanical room
6 Airline office
7 Office
8 In-town check-in counter

0 20m

Perspective at A3 platform

A4 station

A5 station

Research Building, College of Medicine at Fu Jen Catholic University

Design/Completion: 2002/2006
Taipei
47,260 square meters

Fu Jen Catholic University relocated from Beijing to its current site on the outskirts of Taipei 50 years ago as a result of last century's Chinese civil war. After decades of development, the scale of the campus has evolved from a low-density suburb into a highly populated urban environment dominated by mid-rise buildings. The hierarchy of spaces in the College of Medicine extends outward from the historical landmark Chung-Mei Auditorium.

In the new building, laboratories and research facilities are arranged as extensions to each existing department based on proximity. This arrangement helps reduce confusion in wayfinding caused by the complicated building program. A curved glass curtain wall facing the circular plaza spans the old and new sections of the building, symbolizing the school's heritage. It also creates a friendly interface with the entrance plaza, and has since become a new campus landmark.

The program for the new College of Medicine building includes medical laboratories, autopsy rooms, vivarium, clinical trial center, medical library, international convention hall, outpatient clinics and administrative spaces for six departments. The medical library features a spectacular reading area with a view of the outdoor plaza through the three-story glass curtain wall atrium. The second and third floors of the building's west wing are equipped with an extensive environment control system that provides constant temperature, moisture and air pressure controls for individually ventilated rodent breeding cages in the animal labs. The educational autopsy theaters on the fourth and fifth floors are equipped with a specialized ventilation system for disposal of formalin and other airborne chemicals.

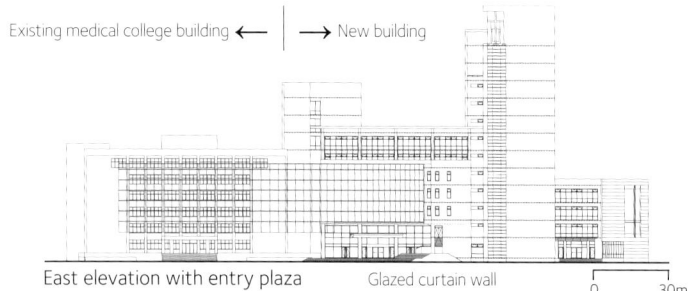

Existing medical college building ← | → New building

East elevation with entry plaza   Glazed curtain wall   0   30m

輔仁大學

Non-glazed ceramic tiles on the building façade and the glass curtain wall give the building a sense of lightness. The perforated metal panels on the building's north and south wall screen off the exhaust ducts from the laboratories. Classrooms with removable maintenance window panels are modeled on the same laboratory module to provide flexibility for future conversion.

Intensive design exercises led to an efficient adaptive reuse of existing buildings and new landmark towers, setting an example for redefining and reorganizing for Fu Jen University campus planning.

The courtyard between the two new towers features terraced seating and doubles as an amphitheater.

The courtyard between the existing and new buildings features an "herbal garden" for medicine related researches.

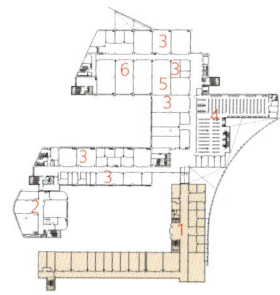

Fourth floor plan

1 Existing medical college building
2 Anatomy research / lab
3 Lab
4 Library
5 MIS mechanical room
6 Administration office

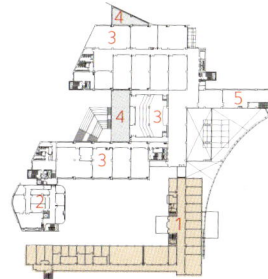

Second floor plan

1 Existing medical college building
2 Animal room (rabbit)
3 Training classroom
4 Patio
5 Lounge

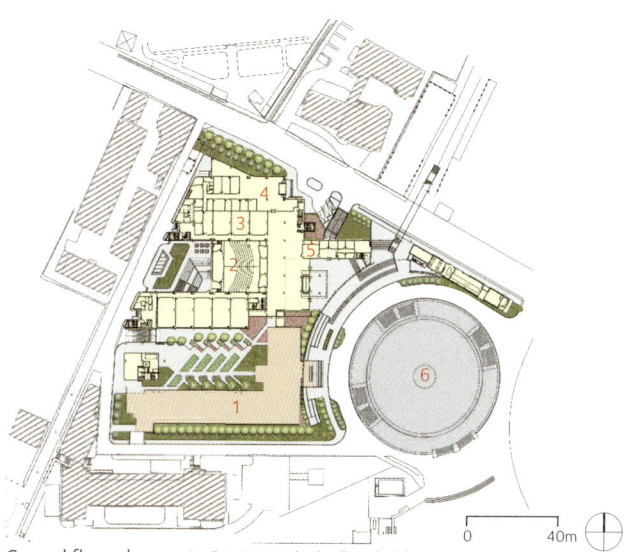

Ground floor plan

1 Existing medical college building
2 Convention hall
3 Classroom
4 Clinic center
5 Office area
6 Chung-Mei Auditorium (existing)

0   40m

School Buildings, Ginling Girls' High School

Design/Completion: 2003/2009
Taipei
18,017 square meters

Ginling Girls' High School reopened in 1956 after relocating from mainland China to a site near the Dahan River in suburban Taipei. After half a century of development, the school is now surrounded by multi-story shopping centers, leaving a 20-meter-wide boulevard facing the riverfront to the south as the only open space along the school's perimeter.

Most of the buildings on campus were aging, prompting the school to start a multi-year redevelopment plan. Through the simultaneous phasing-in of new buildings and rearrangement of open spaces, the original axis started to evolve, triggering a dialogue between the massing and the layers. By raising the outdoor terrace and corridors between new buildings, a new axis with river vistas is introduced to the campus.

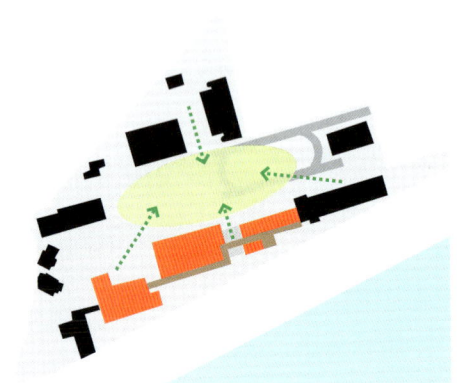

Assembly open space

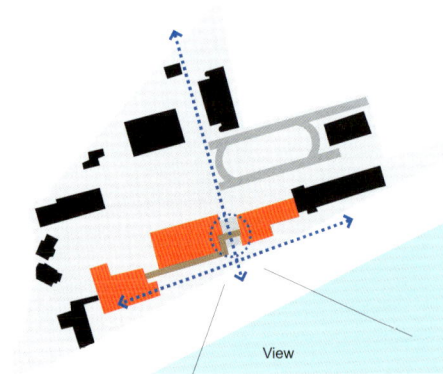

View

Axis

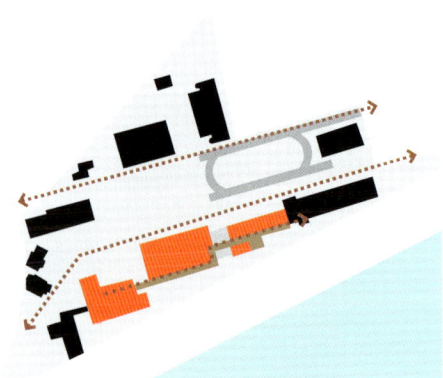

Horizontal circulation

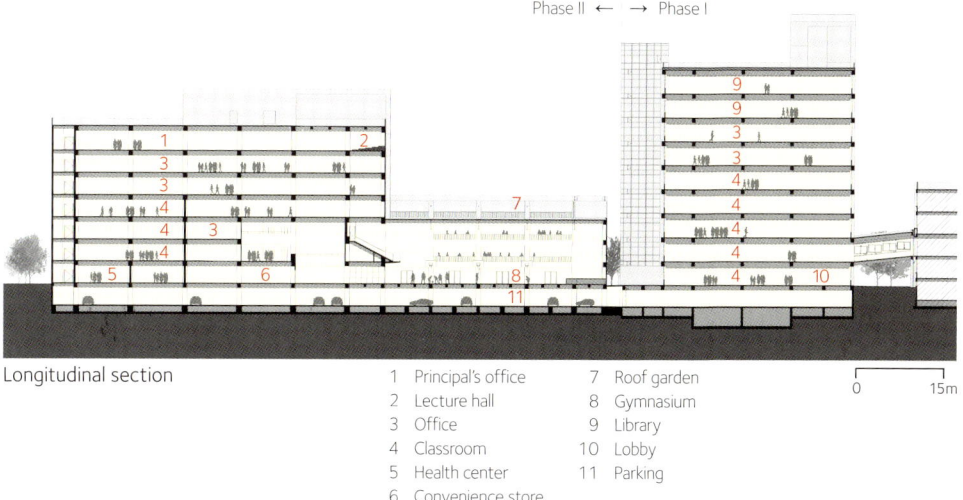

Longitudinal section

1	Principal's office	7	Roof garden
2	Lecture hall	8	Gymnasium
3	Office	9	Library
4	Classroom	10	Lobby
5	Health center	11	Parking
6	Convenience store		

0   15m

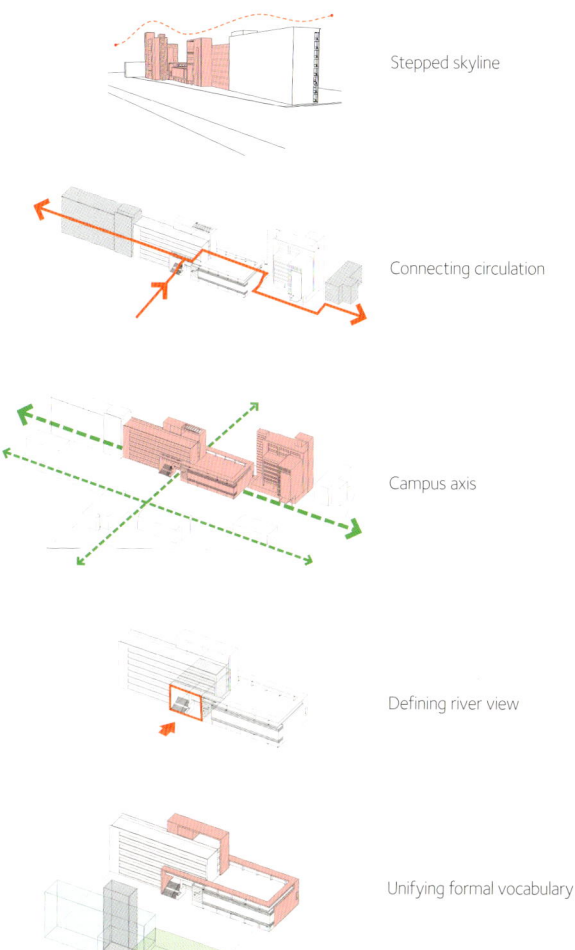

Stepped skyline

Connecting circulation

Campus axis

Defining river view

Unifying formal vocabulary

The phase I building contains a teaching compound with classrooms located on floors one to five. Offices are located on the sixth and seventh floors, while the library occupies the two top floors. The building massing steps down toward the open space in order to alleviate visual congestion at the rooftop gardens while enriching the skyline. A bright, vivacious color scheme works coherently with the brick accent to project an academic image of openness and integrity.

Phase II includes a large gymnasium and the senior high school building. The height of the buildings is 21 meters—a six-meter increase from that of phase one. A new secondary gate adds a connection to the boulevard on the south side of the campus while creating a more harmonious relationship with its surroundings. With its triple-height opening at the corridor, the gymnasium is set apart from the main building to emphasize the north–south campus axis. The gymnasium is three stories high and doubles as a 1300-seat auditorium. The gymnasium's rooftop garden collects excessive run-off during storms and improves the microclimate by minimizing the heat island effect. The landscape design features clean, modernistic geometry, carving through both phases to complement the group of harmonious yet distinctive campus buildings.

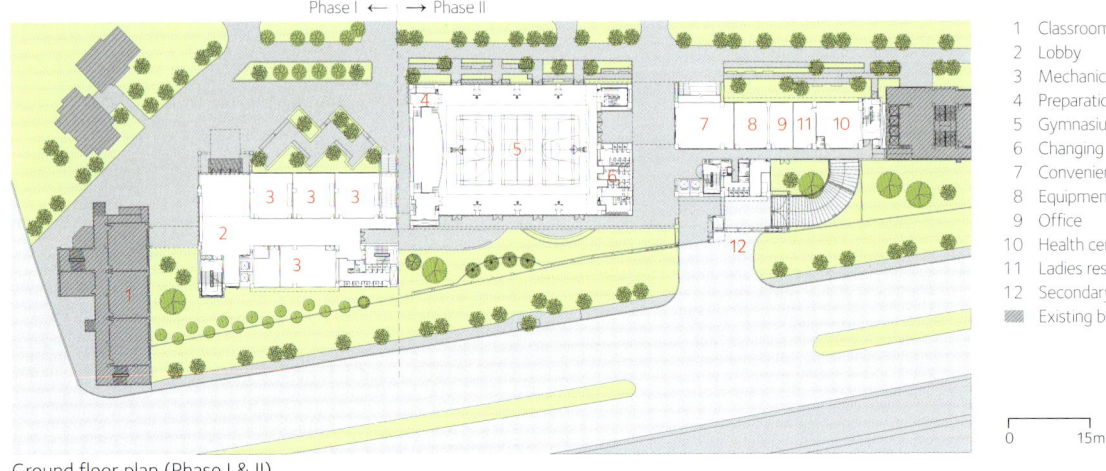

Phase I ← | → Phase II

1 Classroom
2 Lobby
3 Mechanical room
4 Preparation room
5 Gymnasium
6 Changing room
7 Convenience store
8 Equipment room
9 Office
10 Health center
11 Ladies restroom
12 Secondary gate
░ Existing building

0   15m

Ground floor plan (Phase I & II)

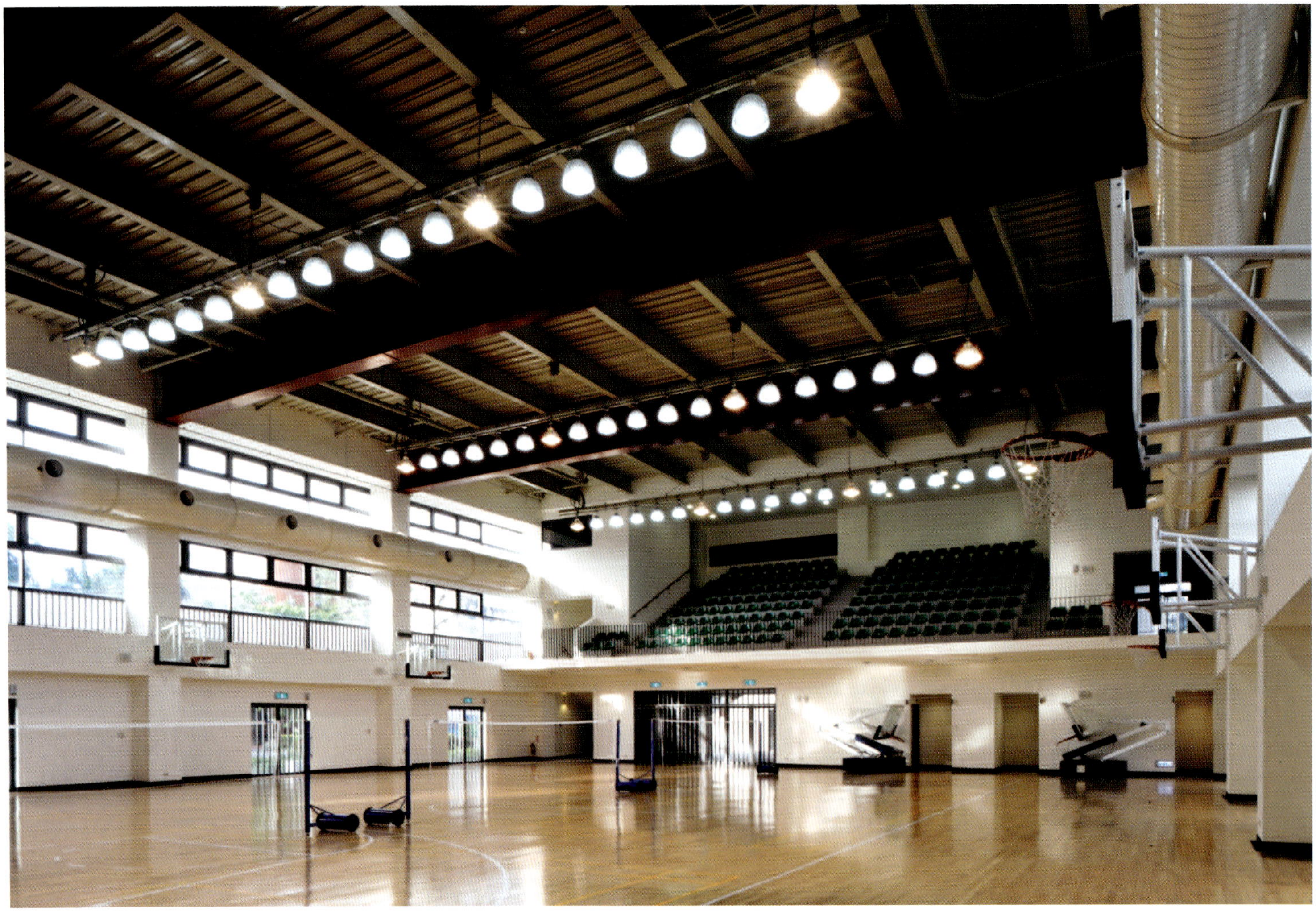

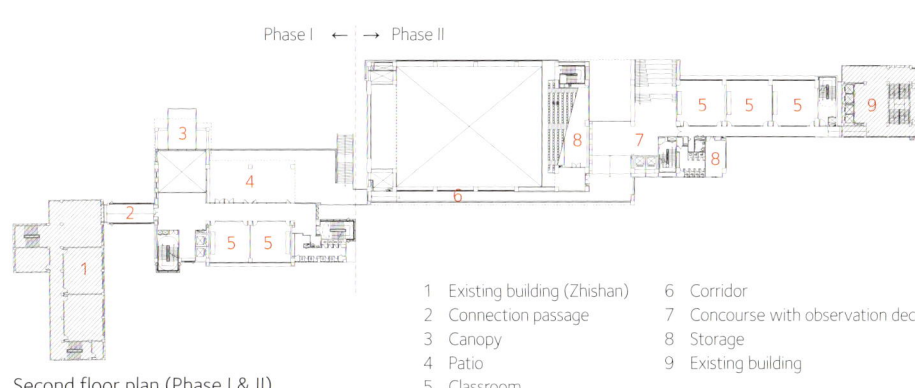

Phase I ← → Phase II

Second floor plan (Phase I & II)

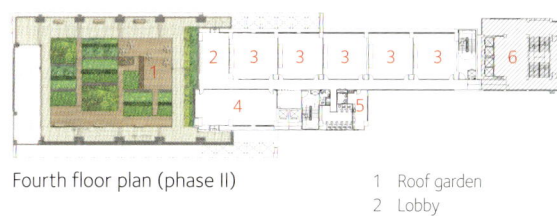

Fourth floor plan (phase II)

1 Existing building (Zhishan)	6 Corridor
2 Connection passage	7 Concourse with observation deck
3 Canopy	8 Storage
4 Patio	9 Existing building
5 Classroom	

1 Roof garden
2 Lobby
3 Classroom
4 Office
5 Kitchenette
6 Existing building

Besides the ornamental and functional benefits, the roof garden also provides a place for relaxation and social interaction.

Research Headquarters, National Chengchi University

Design/Completion: 2009/2012
Taipei
15,970 square meters

National Chengchi University is famous among Taiwan's higher education institutions for its research and development in the fields of humanities and social sciences. With more than 80 percent of the campus situated on the hillside, most of the teaching/research buildings are concentrated on the remaining flat parcels of land to the north. The 1.2-hectare project site is an exception, set apart from the other buildings on the southern slopes of the campus. Situated on the highest point of the existing campus axis, the site also commands a panoramic view. To highlight the Research Headquarters' main role—psychology studies—black and white massing is used as a metaphor to illustrate the relative and complementary relationships among various psychological disciplines. The building layout aims to encourage interaction between the researchers of various backgrounds.

Two asymmetric U-shaped masses are laid out in accordance with the natural topography while taking into consideration the interior functions and floor height. Facilities on the north western side are planned for humanities studies, and those on the south eastern side for psychological research. Classrooms are clustered around two atriums, each with its own distinct character, facilitating vertical movement between different floors. The wider sections of corridors serve as public areas for informal gathering and discussion.

The fenestrations are designed to balance the need between viewing and sun shading. To contrast the boxed windows on the humanities building, the science building features recessed punch windows. All north–south façades feature large fenestrations to allow for maximum natural light and vistas. A lounging platform on the ground floor extends from the central courtyard toward the cherry grove to the west. On the north side, the 200-seat auditorium is shaped as a polygonal mass, symbolizing the solid nature of *veritas* (truth).

········· Campus main gate
▲ Campus axis

Site of new research headquarters building

0   200m

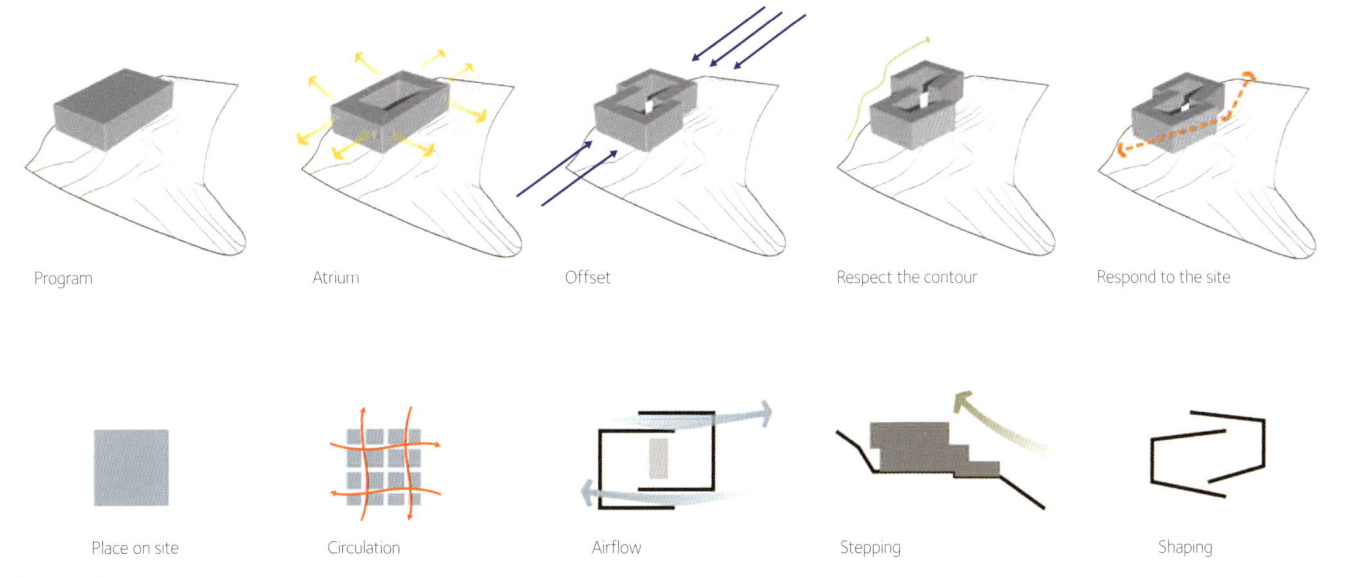

| Program | Atrium | Offset | Respect the contour | Respond to the site |

| Place on site | Circulation | Airflow | Stepping | Shaping |

Concept diagram

The visual contrast between the humanities and science buildings is achieved by different window types and cladding colors.

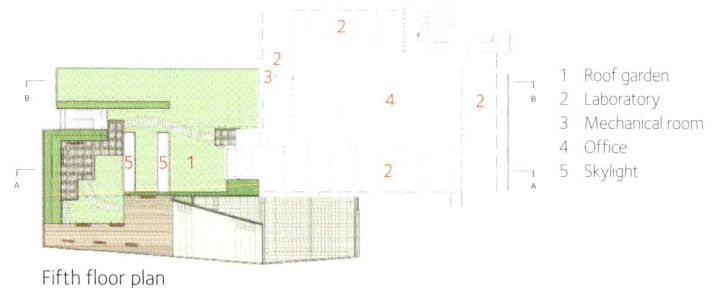

Fifth floor plan

1 Roof garden
2 Laboratory
3 Mechanical room
4 Office
5 Skylight

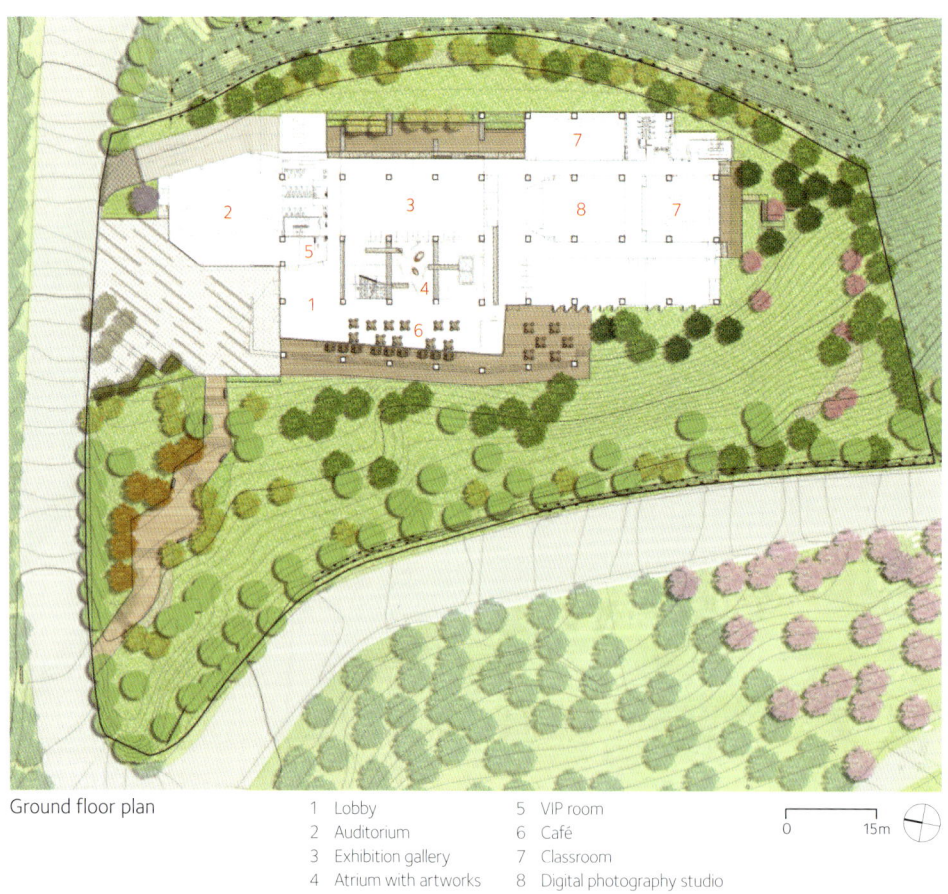

Ground floor plan

1 Lobby
2 Auditorium
3 Exhibition gallery
4 Atrium with artworks
5 VIP room
6 Café
7 Classroom
8 Digital photography studio

0   15m

Both the humanities building and science building have access to the roof garden on the fifth floor. Clerestories are utilized to introduce natural daylight and ventilation, markedly improving the indoor environment. The roof also serves as a rainwater catchment system, reducing the dependence on potable water for irrigation.

Landscaping on the greenbelt ensures the survival of native foliage. In consideration of sustainability, porous wooden planks are used to pave the scenic walkway to attract insects and birds, maintaining the indigenous hillside biodiversity.

Section A

1	Lobby	6	Roof garden
2	Atrium with artworks	7	Classroom
3	Exhibition gallery	8	Conference rooms
4	Meeting room	9	Parking garage
5	Laboratory		

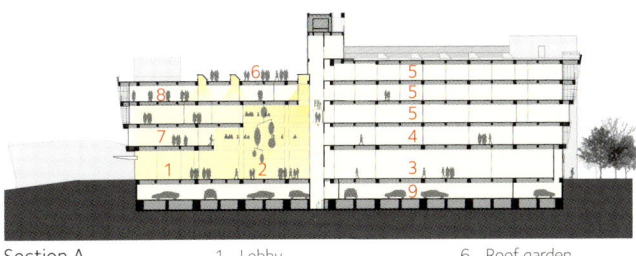

0   15m

Section B

1	Presentation atrium	6	Laboratory
2	Exhibition gallery	7	Office area
3	Digital photography studio	8	Mechanical room
4	Classroom	9	Parking garage
5	Auditorium		

Ningbo Industrial Design & Creative Center Project

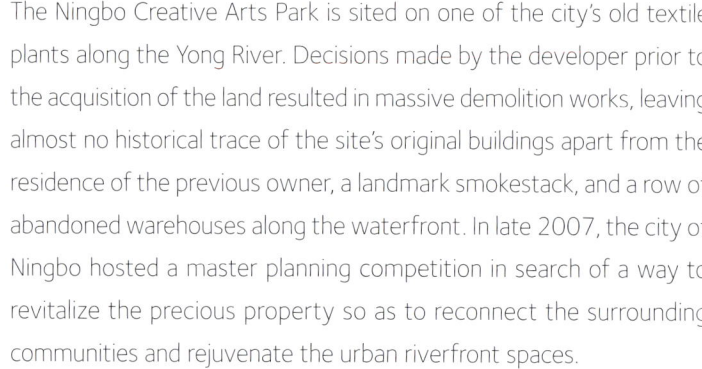

Design: 2007, competition entry
Zhejiang, China
78,000 square meters

The Ningbo Creative Arts Park is sited on one of the city's old textile plants along the Yong River. Decisions made by the developer prior to the acquisition of the land resulted in massive demolition works, leaving almost no historical trace of the site's original buildings apart from the residence of the previous owner, a landmark smokestack, and a row of abandoned warehouses along the waterfront. In late 2007, the city of Ningbo hosted a master planning competition in search of a way to revitalize the precious property so as to reconnect the surrounding communities and rejuvenate the urban riverfront spaces.

The proposed plan started with the idea of reconstructing buildings in a layout that traced precisely the footprint of the original factories on the site. Since an ordinary design approach would result in a massive construction, blocking visual and physical connections linking the waterfront and residential neighborhoods behind, the balance between historical representation and contemporary urbanity presented a major challenge to the design team.

The design proposes a triangular building complex with segments containing creative art studios embracing a center courtyard built around the old mansion. By referencing the historical context, the design pays homage to the site's past. Continuous ramps connect three separate studio buildings, leading to a crescendo at the triangle's tip, symbolizing the pursuit of excellence.

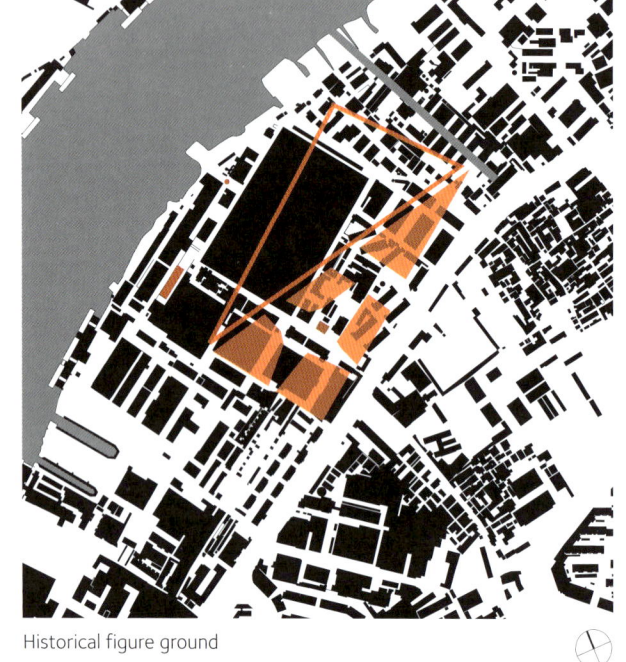

Historical figure ground

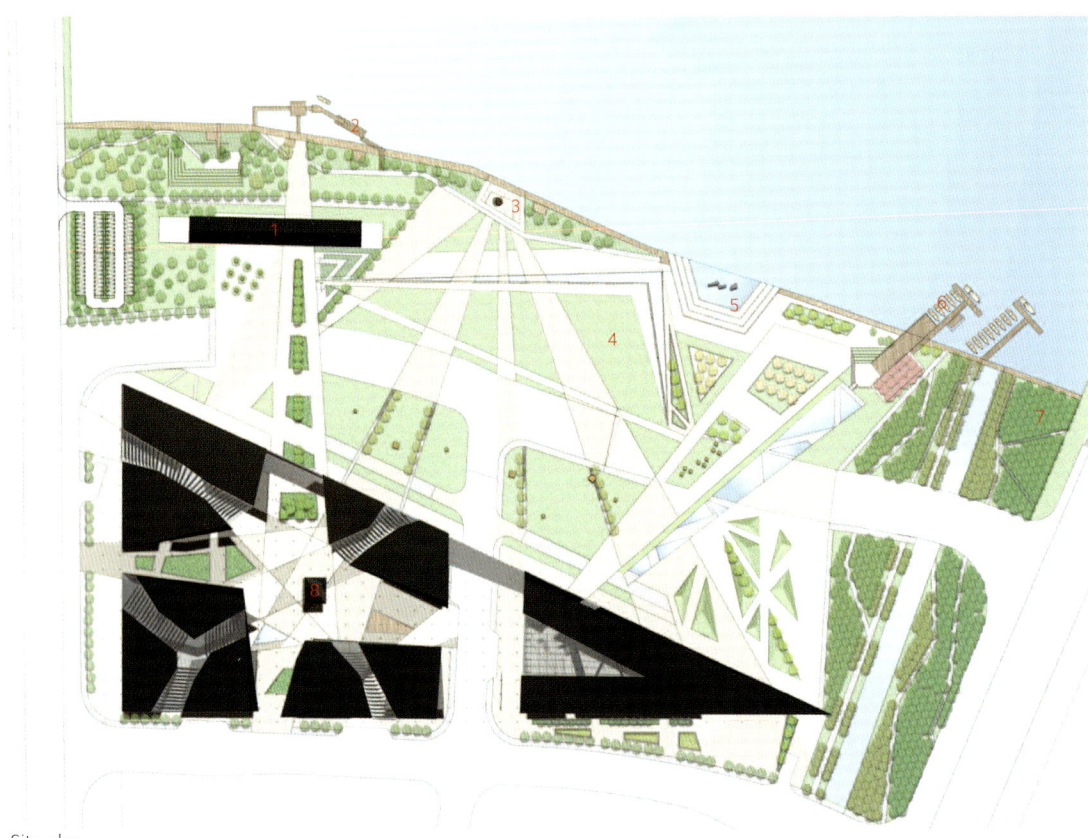

Site plan

1 Existing warehouse
2 River walk
3 Smokestack plaza
4 Outdoor exhibition area
5 Water park
6 Dock
7 Pedestrian trail
8 Memorial hall (old mansion)
■ Main exhibition center

0   45m

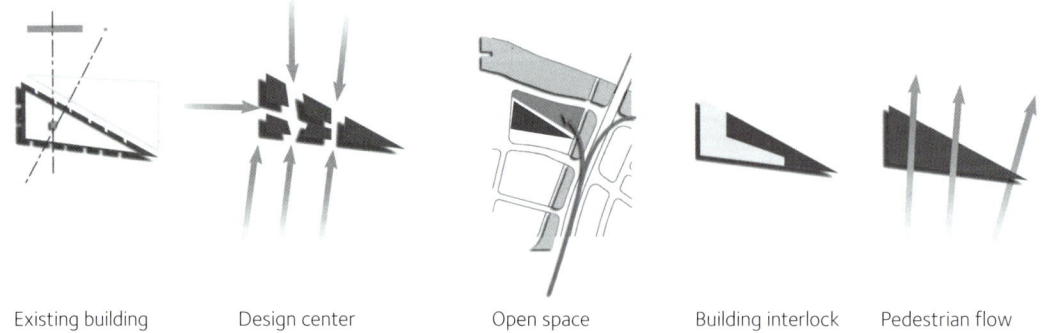

Existing building   Design center   Open space   Building interlock   Pedestrian flow

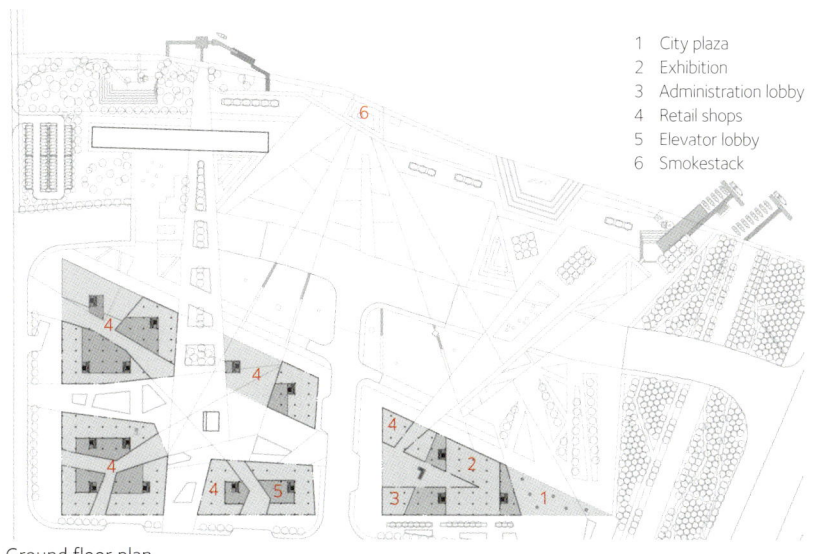

Ground floor plan

1 City plaza
2 Exhibition
3 Administration lobby
4 Retail shops
5 Elevator lobby
6 Smokestack

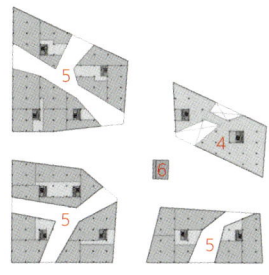
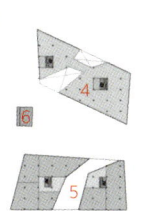

Typical office floor plan

1 Administration
2 Data center
3 Design library
4 Exhibition hall
5 Office
6 Existing mansion

0   45m

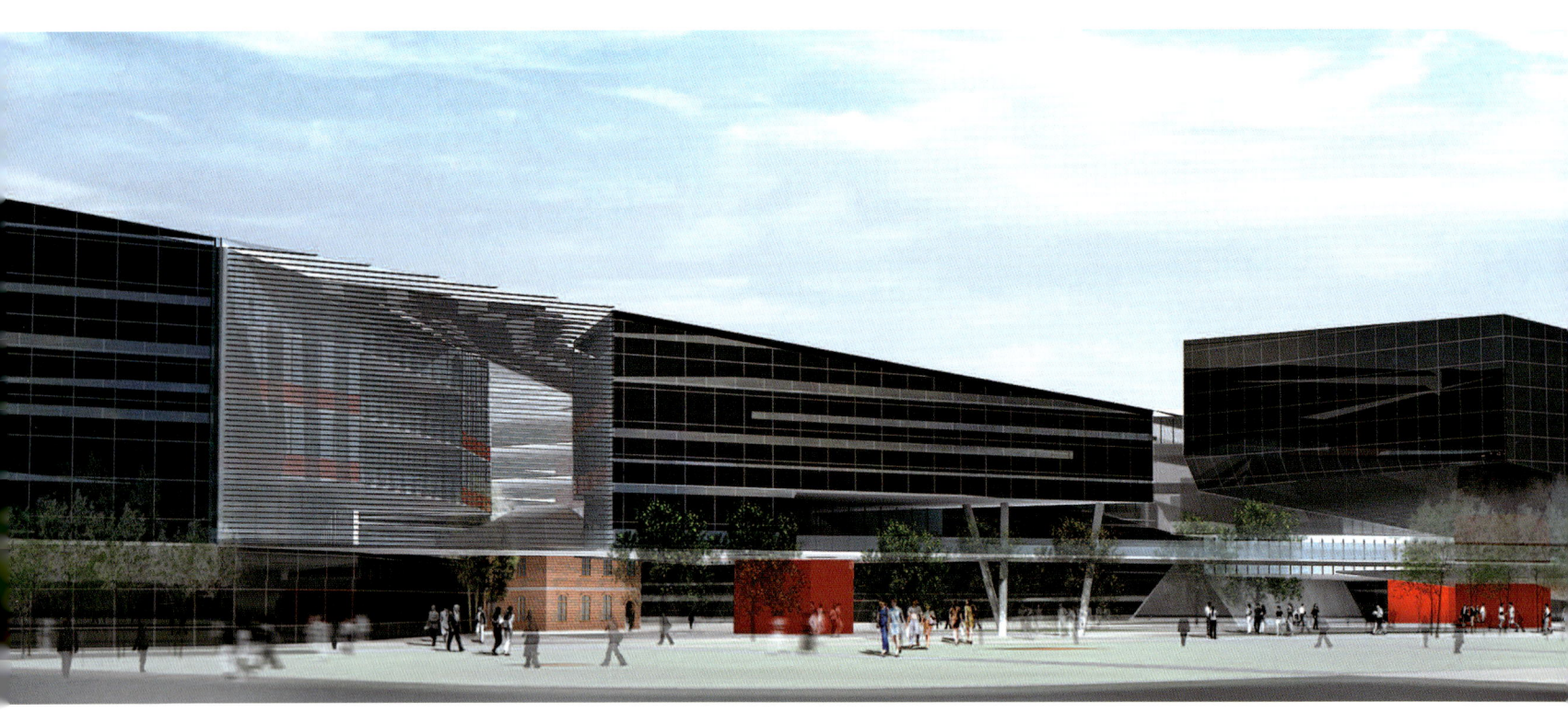

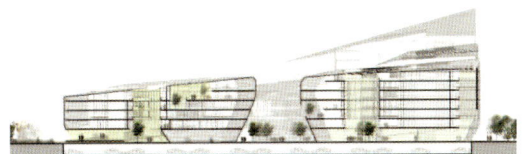

The building height descends in gradual increments towards the river. The administrative office is strategically placed at the apex of the triangular building in an attempt to celebrate the project's pioneering status as a government sponsorial cultural institution.

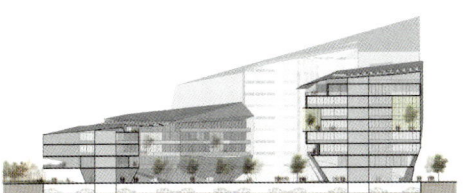

The landscape design radiates out from the landmark smokestack, creating a secondary system stringing together the waterfront circulations and the riverbank warehouses as well as restaurants and art shops in the park. The smokestack's existence symbolizes a major milestone of China's industrial development since the 19th century. The building's triangular tip leads to a focused façade, gesturing towards climactic grandeur.

Section elevations

0   40m

Stockholm Library

Design: 2006, competition entry
Stockholm, Sweden
29,162 square meters

The design competition program called for a new library adjacent to the existing one designed by Erik Gunnar Asplund, now listed as a Grade One historical landmark. The brief specifically asked design entries to fully respect the existing library in terms of its significance in the history of modern architecture while making its own symbolic statement.

The massing of the new library begins with a humble strategy to create a volume identical in length, width and height to the existing library at the point of their adjacency. The design of the new library was then conceptualized as interplay of new versus old, transparency versus opaqueness, decentralization versus centralization, and public domain versus private usage.

The main conceptual framework behind the new library was to provide a circulation system that encourages flow and visibility when moving through the space within. A double helix ramp system was introduced to not only separate the public visitors from the library administrators, but also maneuver people from floor to floor via a pedestrian system that seamlessly and effortlessly connects various programs through one continuous ribbon-like path.

The double helix concept was also applied to the floors, where one level is provided to serve the general public while the other is reserved for the daily operations of the library staff. The curtain wall on the exterior also reflects the alternating public and private realms.

The design for the new Stockholm library complements the existing library by mirroring its massing while contrasting with it in terms of concept. It not only fully respects and integrates Asplund's design, but also makes a statement of its very own, signifying a new way of reading in the 21st century.

Site plan
1 Existing entrance
2 Existing library
3 New entrance
4 New library
5 Annex building
6 The Swedish Institute for Children's Books

0   40m

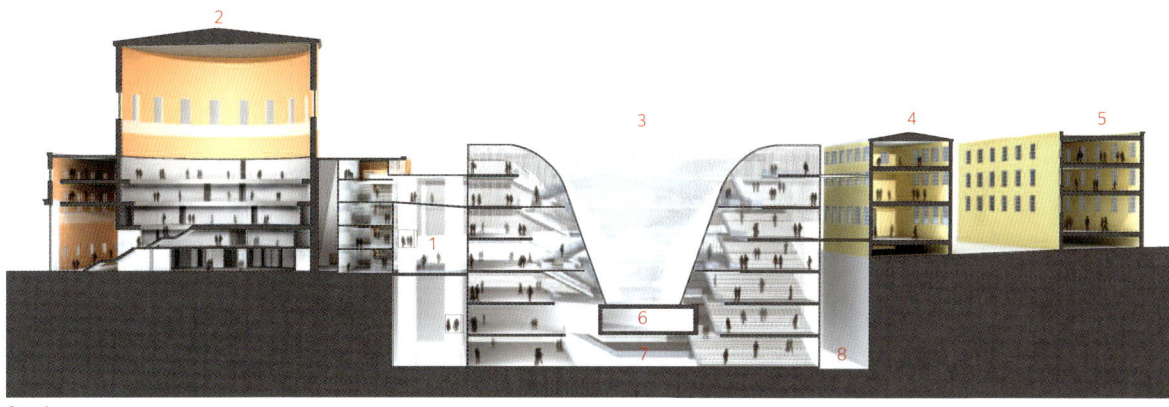

1 New entrance lobby
2 Existing library
3 New library
4 Annex building
5 The Swedish Institute for Children's Books
6 Subway tunnel
7 Auditorium
8 Cafe atrium

0 10m

Section

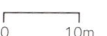

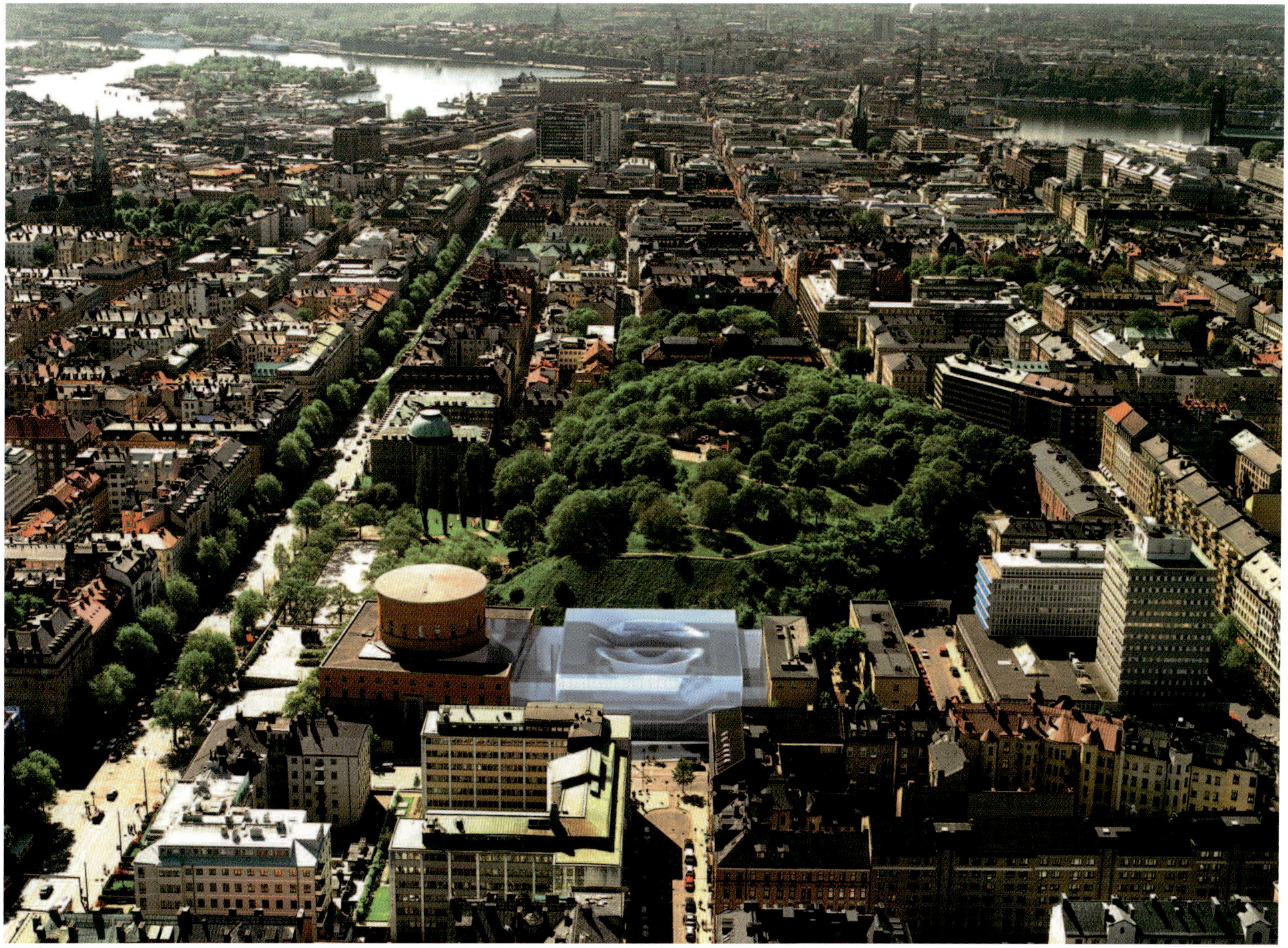

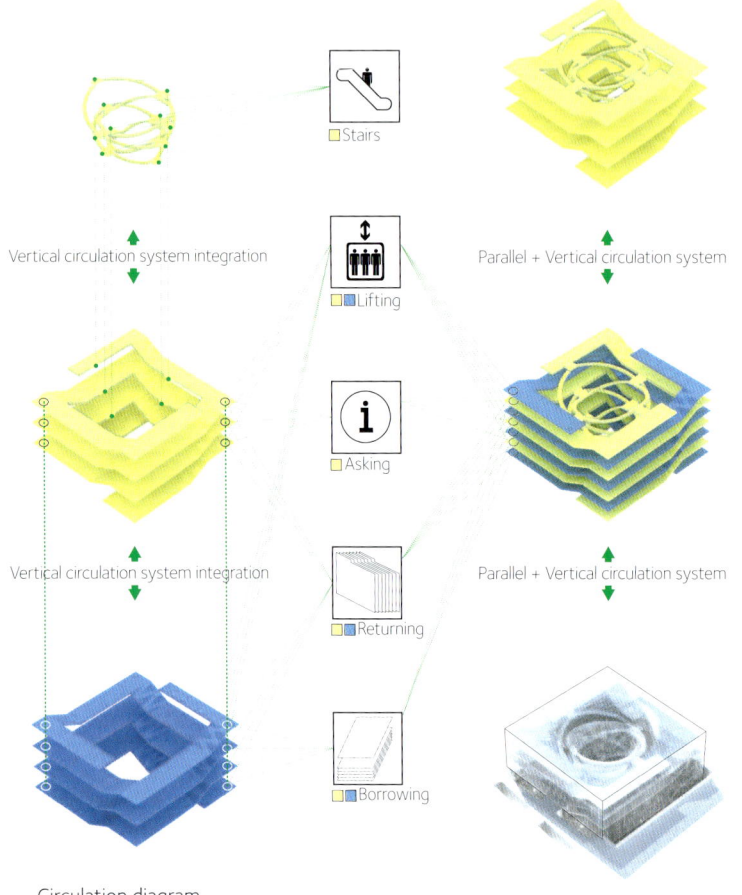

Stairs

Vertical circulation system integration

Lifting

Parallel + Vertical circulation system

Asking

Vertical circulation system integration

Returning

Parallel + Vertical circulation system

Borrowing

Circulation diagram

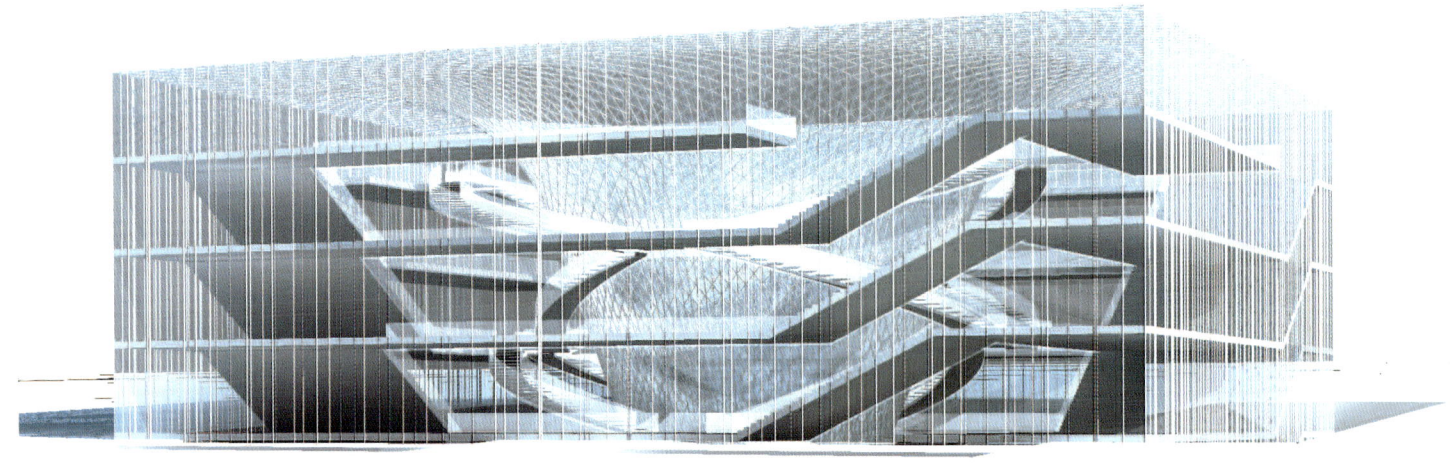

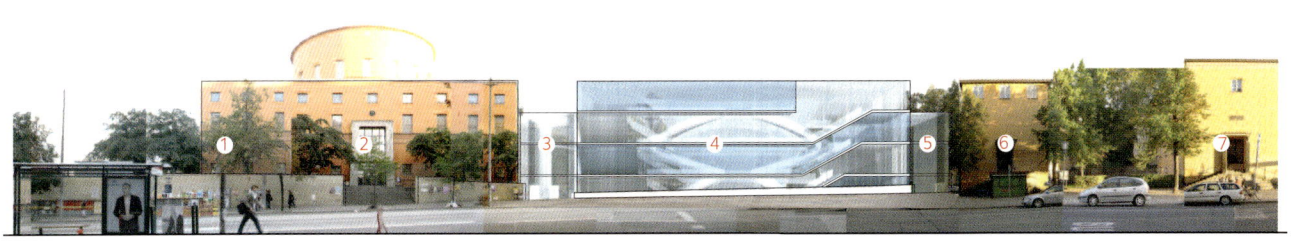

South elevation

1 Existing library
2 Existing entrance
3 New Entrance
4 New library
5 Cafe atrium
6 Annex building
7 The Swedish Institute
  for Children's Books

0   10m

Entry perspective

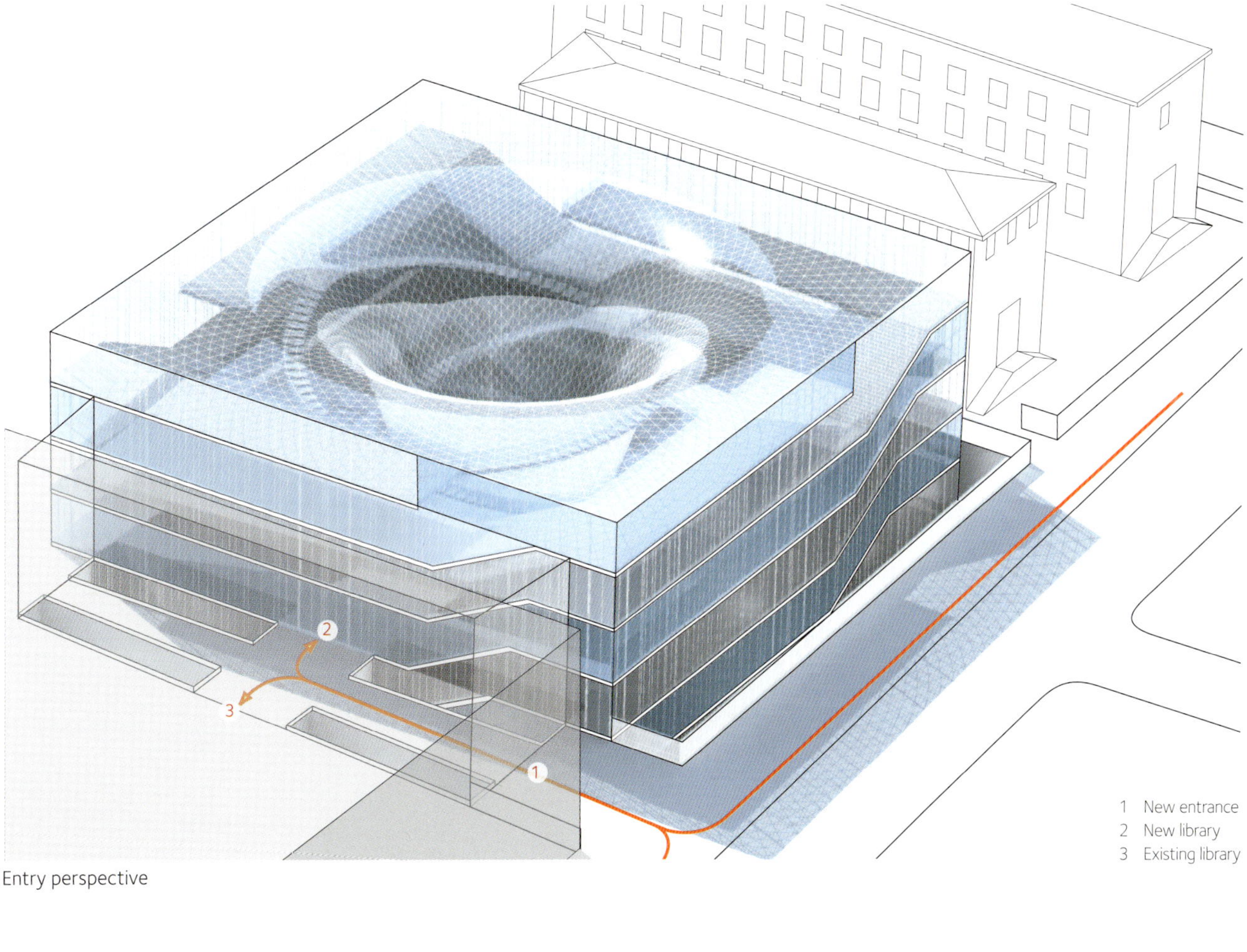

1 New entrance
2 New library
3 Existing library

HTC R & D Project

Design: 2009, design proposal
Taipei
55,200 square meters

HTC Corporation is a premier global innovator and manufacturer of mobile communication devices. The company intends to create a headquarters that reflects the cutting-edge technology it produces.

The tower is configured at a slight angle off the elevated-highway overpass ramp in order to relieve congestion at the main entrance. Space inside the building is articulated in three functional groups above the ground level: the "Agora" at the building base, contains conference rooms, exhibition hall and gym; the "Studios" consist of offices and design houses in the middle section; and the "Executive Floors" are for the corporate directing officers at the top. In between these spaces sits the "interaction zone," including circulation area, staff lounges, vertical greenhouses, a gymnasium, a staff canteen and multi-floor atriums used for important marketing events such as new product premieres and staff gatherings.

One of the most important planning issues for the research and development offices is to physically separate the project teams while maintaining interoperability, allowing the teams to group together to efficiently perform specific tasks when needed. To facilitate the efficient layout, a long-span structural system enabling an open floor plan suitable for teaming and grouping is utilized. Lounges and vertical gardens are strategically arranged in the atriums to promote staff interaction between floors.

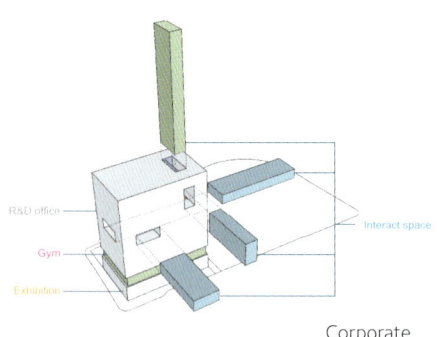

Corporate

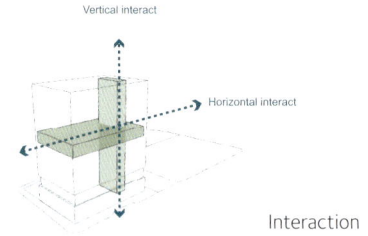

Interaction

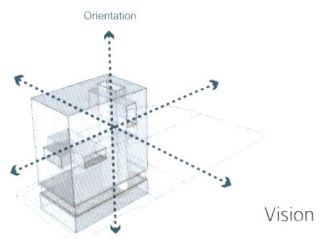

Vision

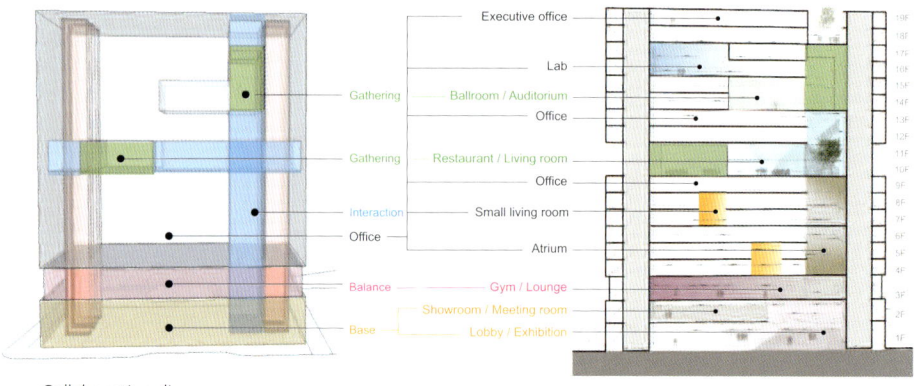

Collaboration diagram

Ground floor plan
1 Entry plaza
2 Interactive landscape
3 Spiritual garden

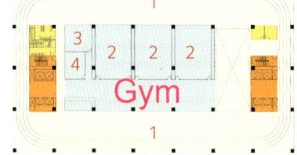

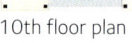

Second floor plan
1 Running track
2 Classroom
3 Women's locker room
4 Men's locker room

10th floor plan
1 Restaurant

14th floor plan
1 Town hall
2 Meeting room

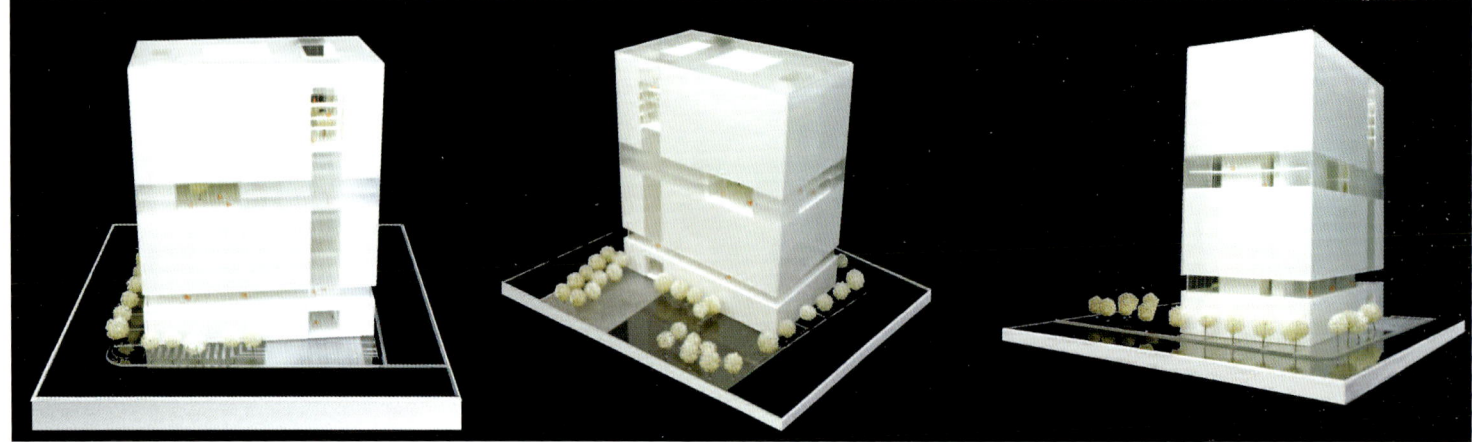

The selection of façade materials also presents a challenge to the design team. The client requires the exterior studio and office walls to be "iconic," to ensure privacy in order to shield technical innovations, and maintain sufficient transparency for views and for natural light to penetrate. After intensive research and testing, a façade combining channel glass made of low iron (extra clear) and a low-e glazing curtain wall are suggested. The channel glass enclosure will allow light to flow into office and studio areas. Within the "interaction zone," the full-height transparent glazed wall provides maximum connection between the interior and exterior, symbolic of the company's global corporate vision. The composition of these two distinctively different kinds of glass elegantly expresses the company's values.

Quanta Display Inc. (QDI) R & D Center Project

Design: 2003, design concept
Taoyuan, Taiwan
88,234 square meters

QDI's R & D center is intended to provide the company's research team with facilities to develop cutting edge technology in sync with the company's ambitious branding campaign. To achieve this, a non-conventional floor plan with maximum flexibility and supplementary space for group discussion is envisioned.

In a conventional office floor plan, the service core is typically placed in the middle of a building while executive offices and boardrooms are positioned along the perimeter. The hierarchy of space is thus based on accessibility to natural light. The majority of working space is therefore located away from the exterior wall and, consequently, remote from natural light. Through precise simulation and calculation favoring an efficient and healthy working environment, the design team concluded that the maximum distance between the exterior wall of the research offices and the central service core should be 15 meters. Spaces beyond this 15-meter mark are provided with natural light and ventilation through variously shaped light wells. A satisfactory layout was achieved through assigning odd-shaped spaces and awkward corners to the service core, as well as the

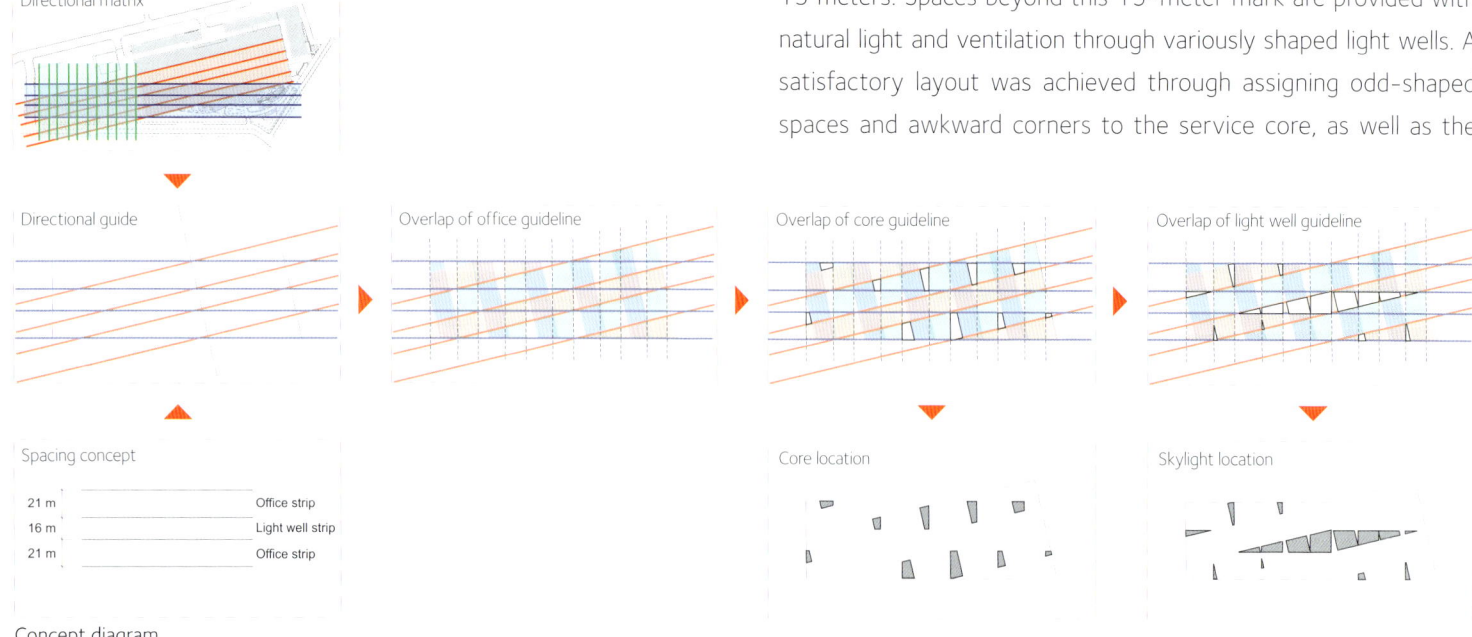

Concept diagram

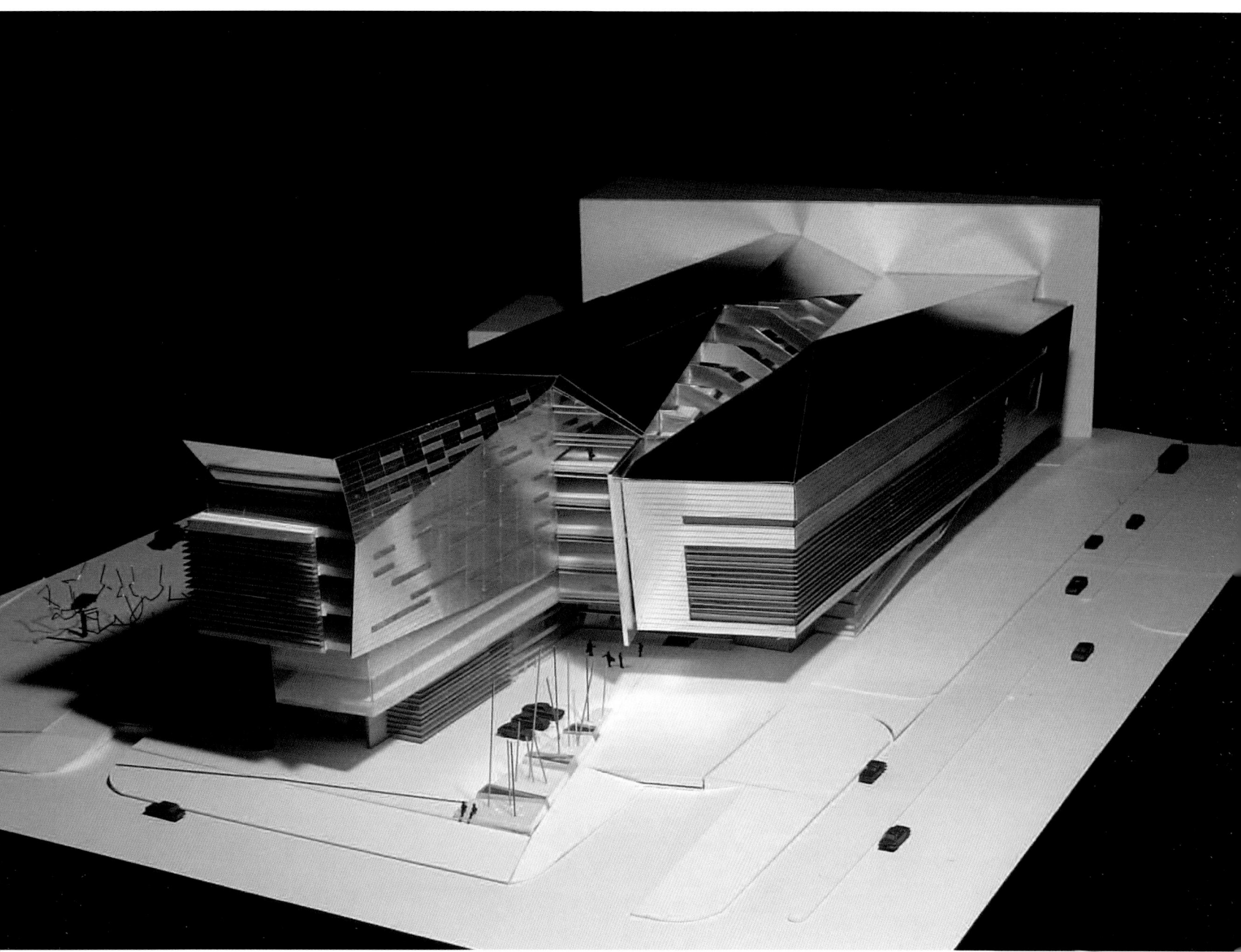

exhibition, recreation and interaction areas, leaving the rest of the building footprint with optimal room for efficiently carrying out office and conference functions.

Utilizing irregular-shaped areas as atriums effectively improves comfort in the working environment while reducing energy consumption. Taking advantage of the large volume of water collected via the water tank in the foundations, a passive heating and cooling strategy is incorporated into the design of the R & D building. Fresh air entering the building through underground ducts is cooled naturally via hydro-geothermal technology and then circulated through the air conditioning system.

In addition to the non-conventional open-floor layout, the innovative structural system creates a vibrant and diverse environment. By freeing up the regular orthogonal column grid and replacing it with shear resisting core walls, the size of columns is significantly reduced. With regard to the building façade, two metal cladding systems for the exterior wall are proposed to achieve a distinctive uplifting visual effect.

The landscape design follows the architectural motif, which applies to the sunken plaza by shaping the outdoor space and echoing the building's overlapped axis and folded skin. As a result, the public space not only blends with the surrounding context but enriches and harmonizes the entire project.

Ground floor plan

1	Main entry	5	Auditorium
2	Employee entry	6	Café
3	Meeting room	7	Exhibition
4	Reception	8	Canteen

Fourth floor plan

1 Cubicle area
2 Office

Fifth floor plan

1 Cubicle area
2 Office

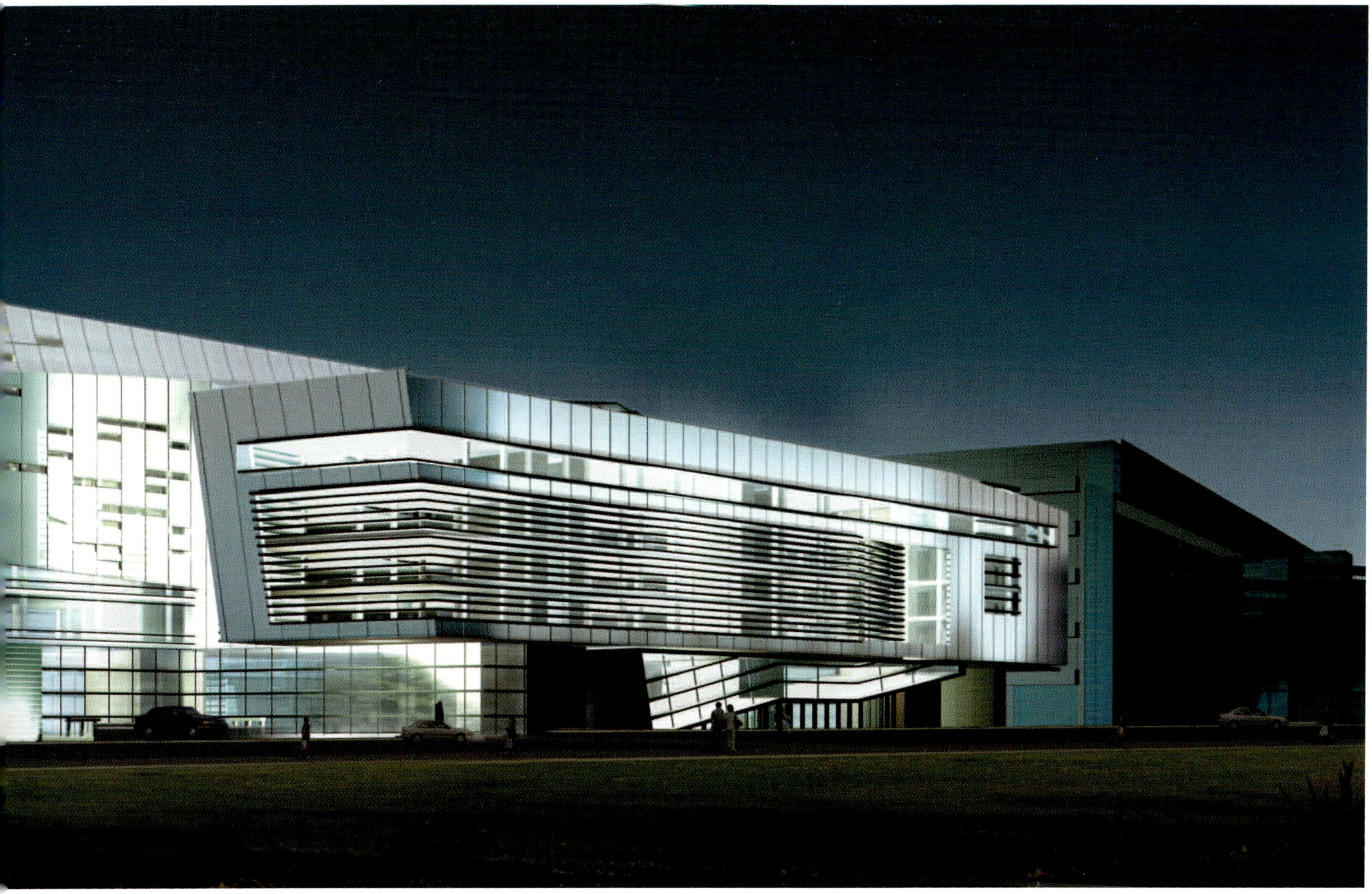

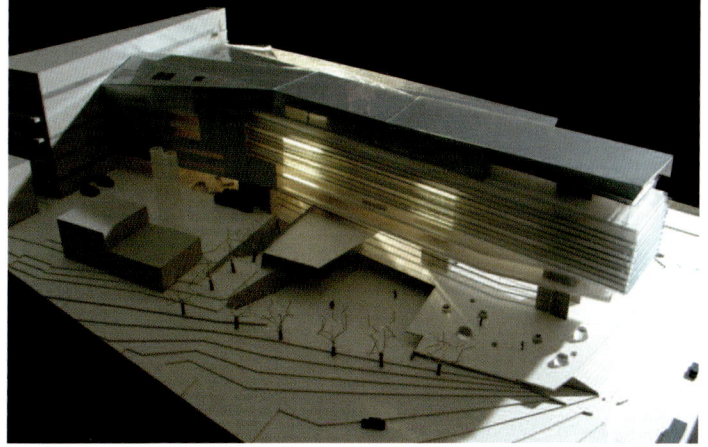

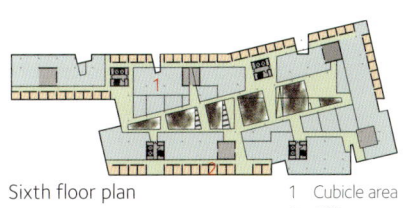

Sixth floor plan

1 Cubicle area
2 Office

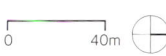

0   40m

Taiwan Dramatic Arts Center Project

Design: 2009, competition, 2nd prize
Taipei
36,190 square meters

The Taiwan Dramatic Arts Center (TDAC) project required the design of two major buildings to accommodate rehearsal and performance space, and serve as the home for four arts organizations: the National Symphony Orchestra, the National GuoGuang Opera Company, the National Chinese Orchestra and the Taiwan National Choir. J. J. Pan and Partners' design draws inspiration from traditional Chinese temple festivals. The space between the buildings is envisioned as an open-air environment to accommodate outdoor performance activities. During the day, artists are encouraged to practice and rehearse in the vibrant, festive atmosphere of the open-air park to attract visitors. At night, the park is transformed into an amphitheater in which audiences are entertained by the performers on stage.

The touring bridge that connects the site to an MRT station offers visitors a leisurely excursion through the traditional Chinese garden. The space below the bridge doubles as an arcade, providing shelter from the rain. The Promotion Center is positioned at the intersection of streets in order to promptly publicize messages and event information to passing traffic. The amphitheater also allows outdoor events to take place in the court. During music festivals, the plaza comes alive with fans and visitors experiencing the diversity of music and drama.

The new center is set to become a leading performing arts venue—one of the few in Taiwan that has its own resident arts companies. To meet the individual requirements for these art groups, the interior space in the rehearsal building is subdivided into four unique sections. The structural system in the main rehearsal hall employs Vierendeel truss placed asymmetrically to accommodate the staggered arrangement. To further buffer possible interference between main rehearsal levels, small supporting programs are arranged on interstitial floors.

遊 yóu (excursion)

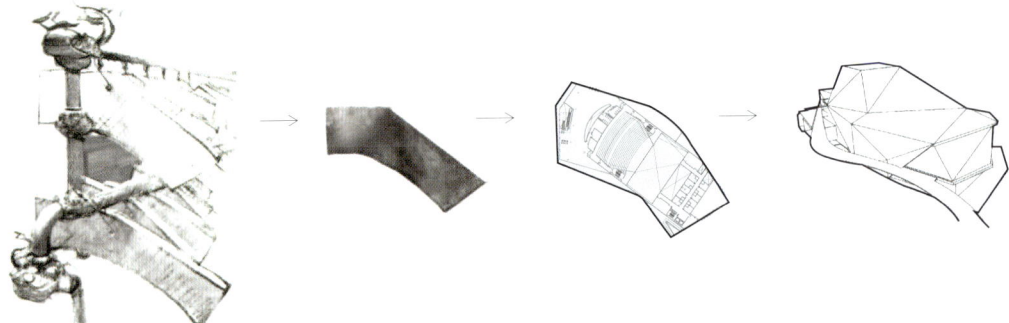

Bianqing, Chinese musical instrument   Chime stone   Floor plan   Building form

The overhung building mass provides shade and forms a backdrop to the outdoor stage while furnishing acoustic reflection to aid the performance of plays. The rear wall of the multi-function rehearsal hall is operable, enabling the space to double as a stage for the outdoor theater when opened. The patio at the rear of the complex stretches out toward a creek, creating a pleasant, leisurely setting for visitors and for artists' morning vocal-training sessions.

The form of the performance hall is modeled on the shape of a "chime stone," a traditional Chinese musical instrument, as well as the geometry of the site. The architectural mass acts as an acoustic buffer to lessen sound disturbance to the adjacent residential building.

Site plan
1 Performance hall
2 Rehearsal hall
3 Promotion center
4 Touring bridge
5 Outdoor platform
6 Bike trail
7 Stepped plaza/
   amphitheater
8 Entry plaza
9 Loading area
10 Overpass
11 Pedestrian bridge

0   40m

The fluid walkway draws design inspiration from Chinese water sleeve dance, taking visitors on a spiritual journey of Chinese performing art.

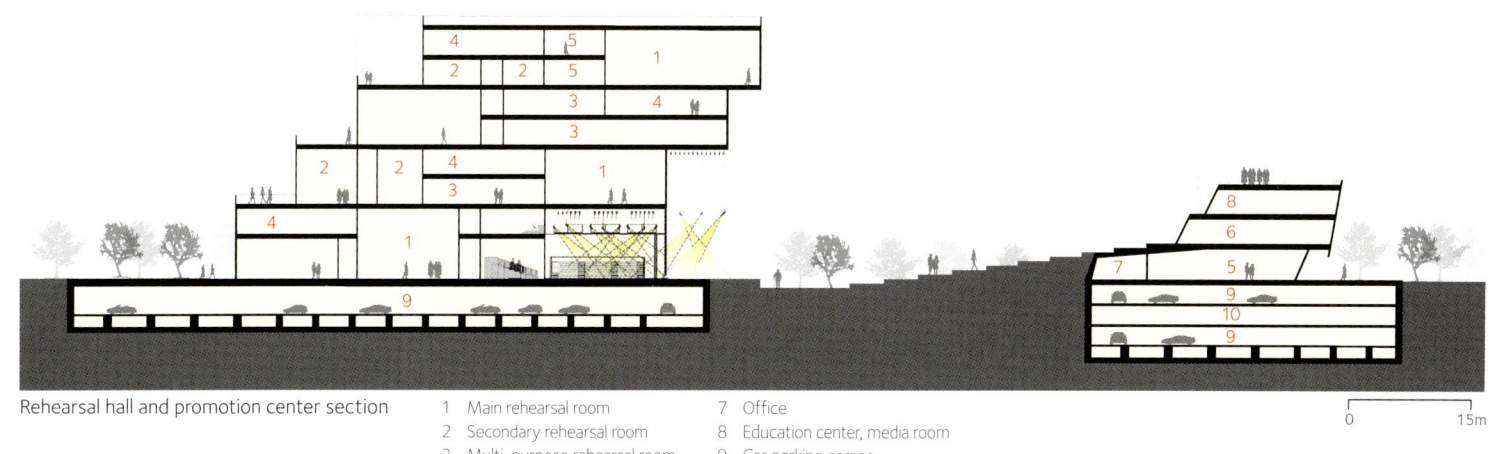

Rehearsal hall and promotion center section

1	Main rehearsal room	7	Office
2	Secondary rehearsal room	8	Education center, media room
3	Multi-purpose rehearsal room	9	Car parking garage
4	Administration office	10	Scooter parking garage
5	Gift shop, gallery		
6	Restaurant		

0   15m

Flagship Building, Huashan Cultural Creative Center

Design/Completion: 2010/2013
Taipei
36,354 square meters
Design concept: competition stage

Situated on the edge of the Huashan Cultural Park, which includes an adaptive reused wine factory to the east, the site is surrounded by multiple historical buildings, a 45-meter smokestack and old warehouses. The redevelopment of this cultural park with a new flagship building aims to provide artists with a base to foster their dreams.

The new building has a floor-to-floor height of six meters, with the ground floor containing designer boutiques and acting as a continuation of the street arcade. The ground level merges into the park to buffer the scale of the city. To accommodate the diversity of uses for each distinctive space, the façade is unified under an organic "cracked ice" pattern. This concept is inspired by the steel truss configuration of old factories, and is reminiscent of the flourishing "caged balcony" commonly seen in local apartments.

An innovative structural system consisting of "braced core" and "Vierendeel truss" is utilized to overcome the 45-meter height limit set by the historical smokestack to the north. By eliminating the conventional columns and deep beams on every other floor, much needed column-free space with extra floor-to-floor height on the ground, third, fifth, and seventh floors is created, to satisfy the space requirements for creative and performing arts activities. On the other hand, the space on the even number floors with vertical truss members can be easily adapted for use as small studio spaces. The combination of the two structural systems enables the building to achieve maximum flexibility as a "platform" to be used for various types of artistic events.

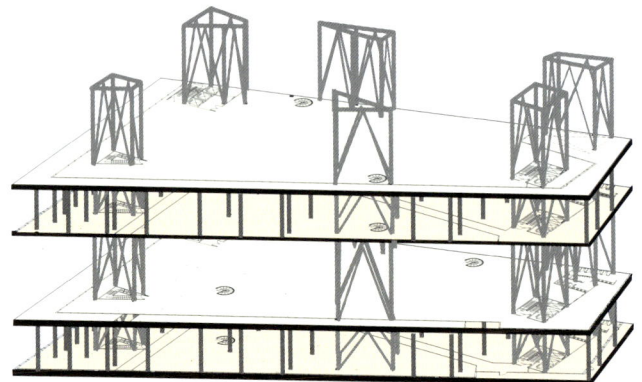
Structural diagram

Site plan

1 BOT
2 Creative space
3 Shop

4 Exhibition space
5 Performance area
6 Entrance plaza

☐ Flagship building

0   60m

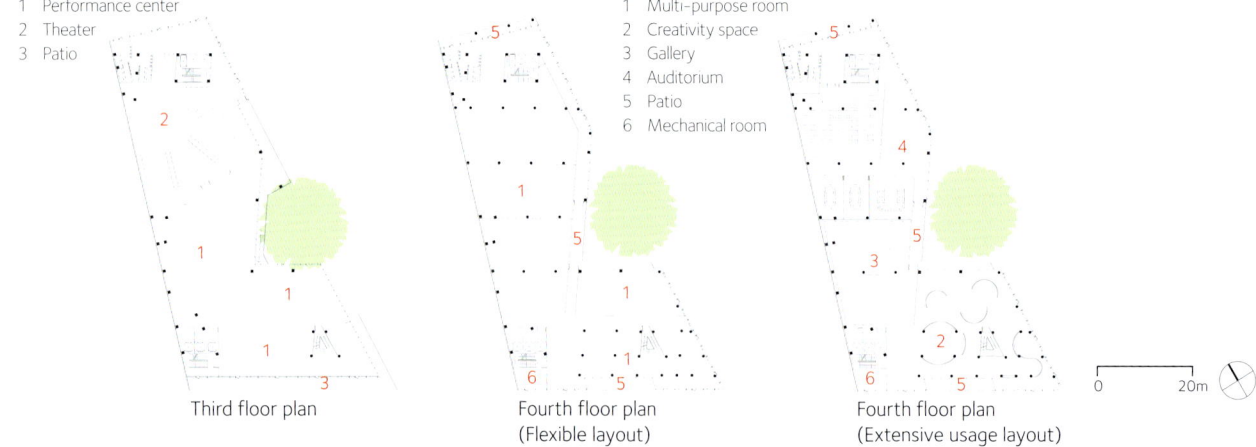

1 Performance center
2 Theater
3 Patio

1 Multi-purpose room
2 Creativity space
3 Gallery
4 Auditorium
5 Patio
6 Mechanical room

Third floor plan

Fourth floor plan
(Flexible layout)

Fourth floor plan
(Extensive usage layout)

0   20m

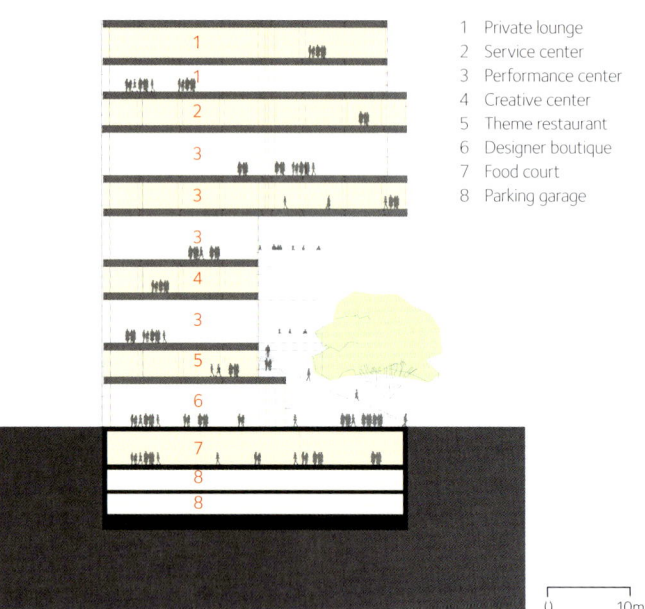

1　Private lounge
2　Service center
3　Performance center
4　Creative center
5　Theme restaurant
6　Designer boutique
7　Food court
8　Parking garage

0　　　　10m

Transverse section

With the roof garden strung together to form a series of linked greenery, the lightweight exterior enclosure blends unobtrusively with the abundance of lush trees in the park. The height is maintained at 45 meters along the north side of the roof to pay homage to the winery's landmark smokestack. By blurring the edge between the interior and exterior spaces, the main plaza in the park becomes an extension of the building, thereby expanding the venue for outdoor exhibitions and performances.

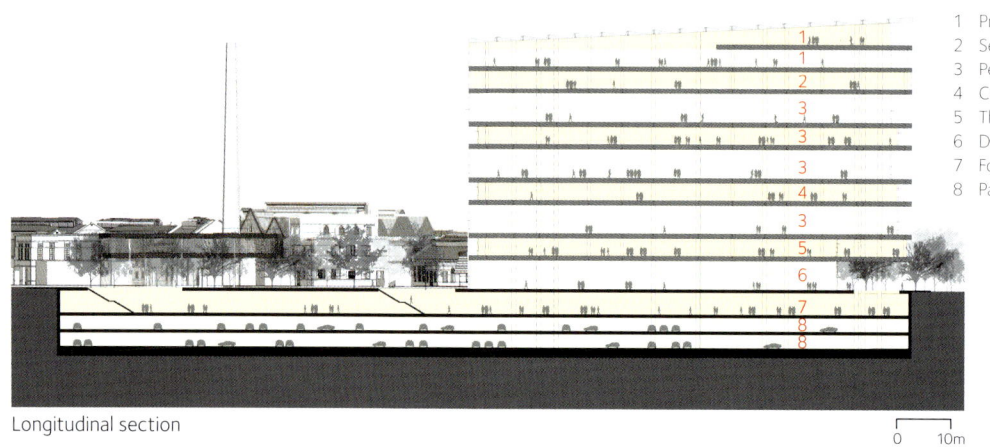

1	Private lounge
2	Service center
3	Performance center
4	Creative center
5	Theme restaurant
6	Designer boutique
7	Food court
8	Parking garage

Longitudinal section

0   10m

An outdoor plaza extends the building to the landmark smokestack and open space beyond.

National Taichung Digital Library

Design/Completion: 2007/2011
Taichung, Taiwan
41,797 square meters

The National Taichung Digital Library exemplifies the "stream of knowledge" connecting literary exploration and urban evolution. Only recently have libraries responded to the digital age by expanding on their traditional role of book lending. However, importance of multimedia interfacing has redefined the National Taichung Digital Library's role as a center of leisure and boundless creative potential.

The facade features a "horizontal flow" theme recalling the excavation of the irrigation canals since the city's early settlement in the 18th century, as well as symbolizing the fluid data interface in the modern information age. The themes in the various reading rooms emulate the dynamic nature of digital media, while skylights and horizontal inclining windows allow in diffused natural light. The interior design motif for each floor takes its cue from the outside view. Standing for the ground floors up, the motifs are bushes, tree -trunk, branches, canopy, the city skyline, and clouds.

The building's free-formed skin is unique in its curved planes and organic tree trunk-shaped columns. A composite wall system with integrated insulation molds the folding surfaces, and the attention to minute details enables the skin to achieve a monocoque appearance. Symbolically, the shifting curves pay tribute to the unique context of central Taiwan's rivers and waterways.

The building's L-shaped form embraces the greenbelt with its sociopetal gesture. The landscape design features a moon-gazing berm with a multitude of native plants and low-maintenance wind-resistant shrubs. An ecological waterway wraps around the site, providing the neighboring community with a joyful image of reflection. The integrated rainwater collection system in the landscape pond, combined with the roof garden, improves the micro-climate and reduces the heat island effect in the heart of the city.

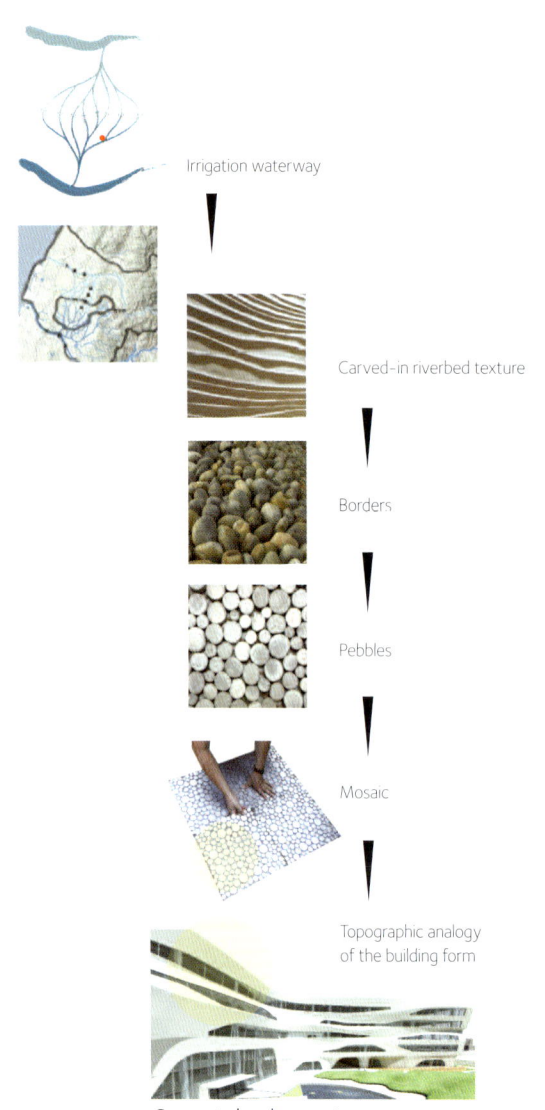

Irrigation waterway

Carved-in riverbed texture

Borders

Pebbles

Mosaic

Topographic analogy
of the building form

Concept development

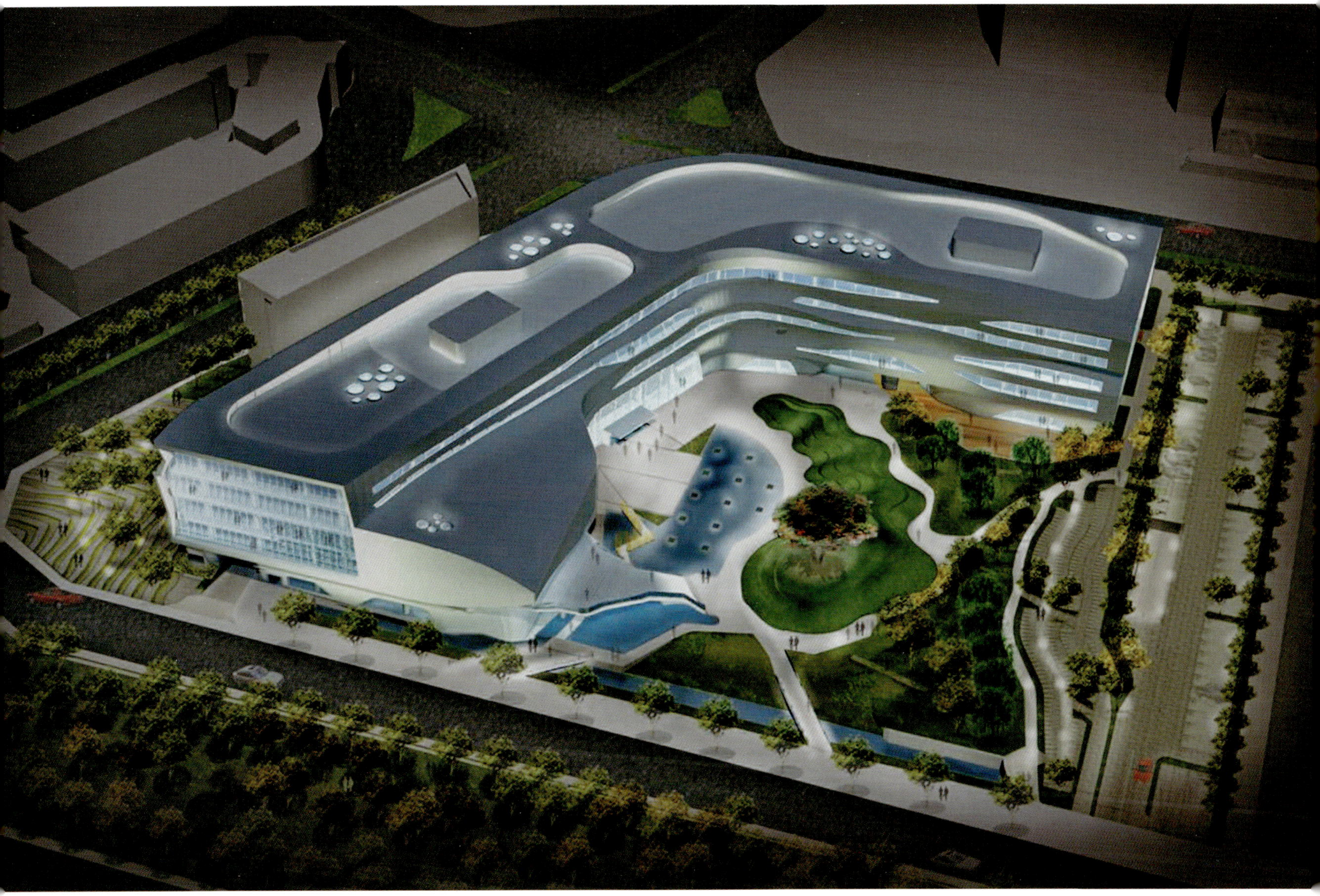

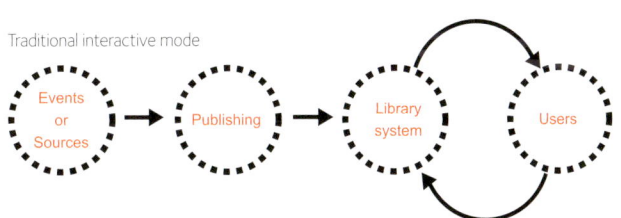

Traditional interactive mode

Events
or
Sources
Publishing
Library
system
Users

Interactive mode in National Taichung Digital Library

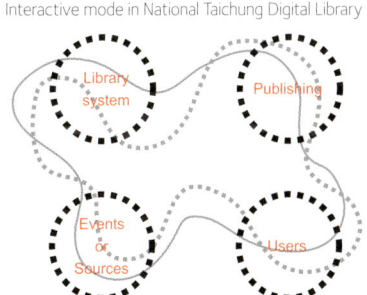

Library
system
Publishing
Events
or
Sources
Users

Design strategy

First floor plan

1. Lobby
2. Digital experience zone
3. Coffee shop
4. Convenience store
5. Bookstore
6. Automated book return
7. Catalogues/Searching area
8. Children's digital center
9. Children's reading zone

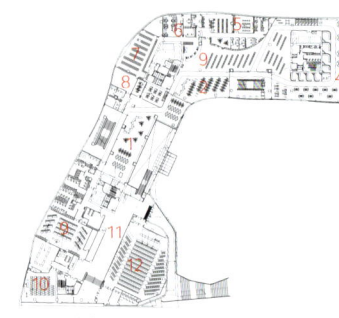

Second floor plan

1. Digital experience zone
2. Internet resources center
3. Multimedia collections zone
4. Audio/Video zone
5. Deaf–blind digital information center
6. Offices
7. Multimedia storage
8. Digital Audio/Video center
9. Conference room
10. Digital learning classroom
11. General exhibition zone
12. International conference hall

1 Reference zone
2 Periodicals
3 Elderly zone
4 City historic information center
5 Multicultural center
6 Classroom
7 Administration zone
8 Audio/Video room

Third floor plan

1 Digital youth center and reading zone
2 Arts zone
3 Languages zone
4 Humanities data zone
5 Administration zone

Fifth floor plan

0   20m

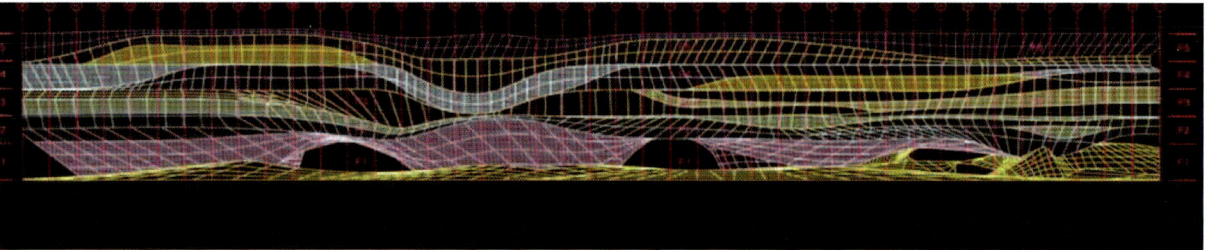

The building enclosure is developed through digitized CAAM process to simulate the visual effects of the carved-in riverbed texture which is commonly seen in central Taiwan.

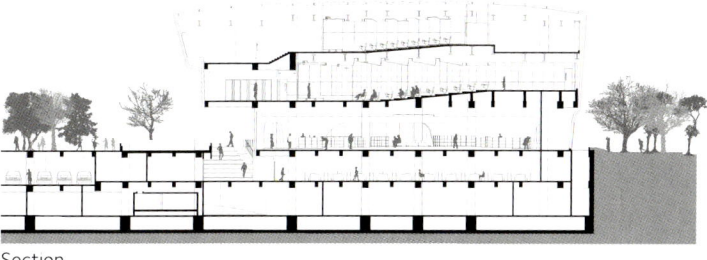

Section

Pass it on

Joshua Jih Pan, FAIA

J. J. Pan and Partners, Architects and Planners is celebrating its 30th anniversary this year. Over the past three decades, we have grown from a three-member workshop into a group of branch and subsidiary companies with a total staff of nearly 300.

Defying the conventions of standard operational practice, the firm has consistently refused to adopt the structure and organization of a traditional corporation. Rather, the practice has maintained the operational model of a design studio, or group of studios, with structural flexibility. This has helped us preserve the intimate personal working relationships between co-workers that are unique and pertinent to small firms, even as we have grown larger in size.

Reflecting back through the years, though it was never intentionally planned this way, the development of our firm can be divided into three decade-long stages: Survival and Establishment of Core Values, Rapid Expansion, and In Search of the Next Step.

The First 10 Years: Survival and Establishment of Core Values

With a staff of two, I started out by undertaking small-scale institutional projects through job interviews and competitions, using the education and professional training I received in both Taiwan and the US. Believing architectural theory and practice to be equally important—not only in enriching an architect's experience, but at the same time providing opportunities for testing creativity, ideas and professional boundaries—I took up a teaching post while concurrently running my architectural practice. Consequently, most of our firm's core staff is talent recruited from the architectural schools I was teaching at.

Our focus in the founding years of the firm was to establish clear design goals and to establish practice standards suited to local construction technology and design guidelines while also trying to improve design standards at every opportunity. My philosophy in architecture has always been to achieve a "total architecture"—for an architectural firm to balance design, service and delivery to its clients.

Establishing a successful reputation through our institutional work and our expertise in combining advanced design with punctual, reliable and high-quality delivery of projects, the firm was able, in the second decade of its development, to enter into the rapidly expanding high-tech industry niche market. This inevitably set the tone for the firm and led to its subsequent expansion and diversification as a result of client requests for the provision of extra services.

The Second 10 Years: Rapid Expansion

J. J. Pan and Partners' design precision, sensitivity to advanced technologies, and punctual management, design delivery and implementation processes—so valued in the high-tech industry—placed the firm in high demand during the I.T. industry boom. Direct and walk-in design commissions mushroomed as the high-tech industry flourished. While catering to the demand for a new building type that was becoming increasingly popular within the high-tech industries, an awareness was growing of the impact these buildings had on limited land areas and tight building sites. The challenge that emerged was how to promptly design and build these typically enormous, rigid volumes while at the same time respecting the surrounding environment and providing a pleasant space for those inside the building and those passing by.

As there were very few comparable reference projects either in Taiwan or abroad, where industrial land parcels are generally much larger in size, we not only had to explore different design possibilities and invent a new building typology, but also persuade clients that the investment in additional construction costs was part of their social responsibility. Instead of treating high-tech industrial buildings as enormous boxes, our critical goal became the creation of distinguished buildings and pleasant environments that differed from the typically bland, mundane manufacturing sheds. This endeavor contributed to the evolution of Taiwan's high-tech industrial buildings as a unique form of architectural typology that is in context with the surrounding urban fabric and is environmentally congenial.

While the growth of the I.T. industry prompted J. J. Pan and Partners to rapidly expand, the firm continued to be involved in the design of other institutional building types, including higher education, healthcare, hospitality facilities and religious buildings. During this period, the increasing need of clients for a "one-stop service" resulted in the firm branching out to include interior design, construction management and structural engineering services. Thus our architecture office began providing integrated services in-house long before cross-disciplinary integration and collaboration became a widespread phenomenon within professional architectural practices.

J. J. Pan and Partners office plan, 2005

J. J. Pan and Partners Taipei office

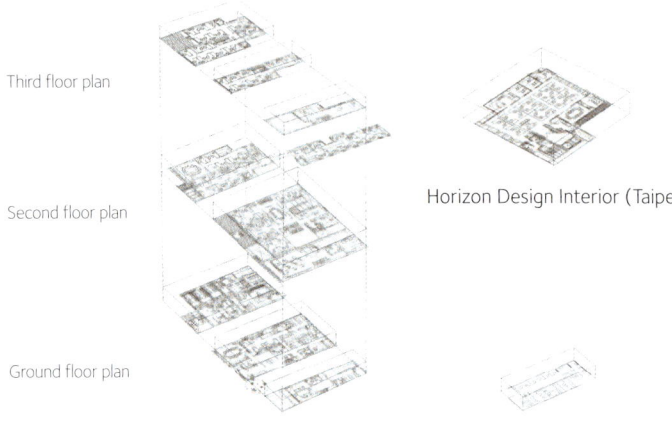

Third floor plan

Second floor plan

Horizon Design Interior (Taipei)

Ground floor plan

J. J. Pan and Partners   TEAM Engineering Consulting

J. J. Pan and Partners subsidiary companies in Taiwan, 2011

Horizon Design Shanghai Office, 2005–2011

The Third 10 Years: In Search of the Next Step

While an integrated design service has become standard practice at J. J. Pan and Partners, striving for design excellence to achieve and sustain timeless value has always been our goal and mission. As our clients expanded their businesses and markets outside of Taiwan, we were requested to provide extended services in various cities in China and the US. With an increased number of senior leaders in the firm and the addition of a select, highly skilled and internationally trained staff, the establishment of branch offices became both a possibility and a natural step in the firm's development. Our Shanghai, Xiamen and Tianjin offices' Horizon Design, were opened in 2001, 2006 and 2007 respectively. These offices inevitably became platforms for the cultivation of leadership, and designated senior officers were dispatched from Taiwan to manage the branches with supporting team members both transferred from Taiwan and hired locally.

As the firm achieved strong and profitable growth, the formulation of a sound succession plan became critical in my mind during this decade. To ensure a sustainable practice, in 2001 I made the decision to change the firm from a sole proprietorship to a partnership. Within this period, in addition to myself, five principals were named and some thirty associates were promoted to jointly manage the firm. The role of managing partner became rotational, thus allowing each principal to become familiar with the operation of the firm. J. J. Pan was no longer simply a personal name, but a brand name, requiring everyone in the firm to share responsibilities, take ownership, maintain design excellence and uphold its reputation.

With the blessing of many dedicated, talented people and an abundance of resources accumulated over the years, I truly believe that J. J. Pan and Partners and its people should not suffer or be wasted simply because of a change in management or the aging or retirement of seniors. A healthy, high-quality firm should be able to sustain itself over time through the emergence and nurturing of new generations of prospective leaders. This does not occur naturally and requires careful planning and nourishing. One of the primary goals for me is to attract, train and develop young talent so that the torch that fosters creativity and the delivery of top-quality design services will be passed on at J. J. Pan and Partners.

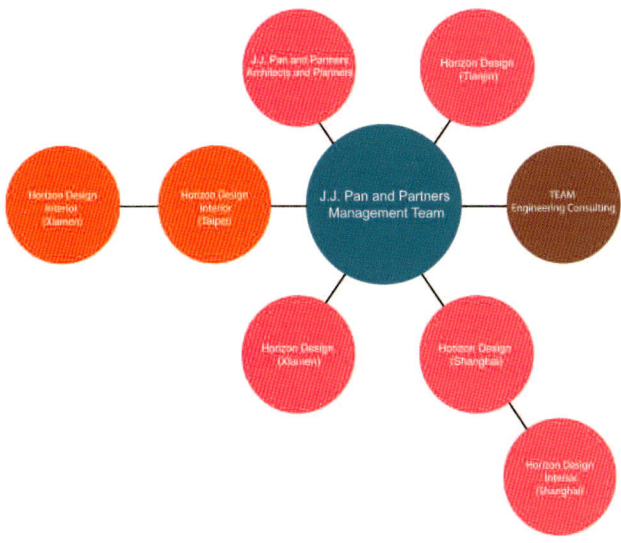

An Organic Office

J. J. Pan and Partners is the largest architectural firm in Taipei. It has branch offices in Xiamen, Tianjin and Shanghai, and interior design and engineering offices in Taipei, with a total of approximately 300 employees. This growth from humble beginnings with a handful of employees is testament to the firm's lasting virtues and ethical practices. But it is J. J. Pan and Partners' unpretentious modus operandi that is its most unique characteristic, stimulating a pleasant working environment and an organic growth that differs to similarly-sized corporations.

Mr. Joshua Jih Pan is the founding principal of the firm, but he also places the operation of the firm in the hands of five other principals who are in charge of different teams based on location, projects and clients. Not only is this configuration an effective office management strategy, it gives Mr. Pan the freedom to do what he enjoys most—that is, contributing to and guiding the firm's designs.

The Taipei main office extends out from Mr. Pan's residence and consists of long, narrow rowhouses, with the office occupying six units sandwiching a longstanding neighbor. The "three plus three" setup promotes separate but interoperable departments. Due to the elongated floor plans, each unit of the office has a level of privacy and intimacy beyond that of a conventional cubicle-based office. Seating arrangements are determined by projects and groups, not necessarily hierarchy, so that principals and associates sit among everyone else within the unit. This configuration breaks down the conventional "corner-office apartheid" and naturally promotes healthy professional relationships. It seems counter-intuitive, but upon further scrutiny the semi-segmented units provide the necessary psychological relief lacking in open offices.

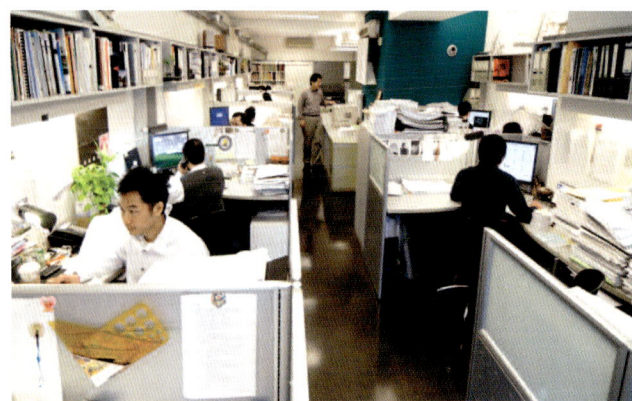

Each department has an associate-in-charge overlooking the work schedules of the group members while at the same time ensuring the most efficient performance. This responsibility includes the management of man-hours and project hours, communication between the groups and group members, as well as assigning members to suitable projects. Most importantly, the associates act as the main communication representatives within the firm, both vertically and horizontally; and this requires both highly effective communication skills and the ability to maintain impartiality. Employees often transfer within the office to gain experience on different projects. The associates allocate personnel based on their skill set and attributes, and not just for the sake of scheduling. This promotes efficiency and camaraderie in the office, as well as high quality projects.

The firm expanded into China following requests from clients who wanted services provided locally. As the company's profile grew, it was a natural progression to set up offices in strategic locations in China in order to take advantage of the thriving market. The entire firm, including the offices in China, shares the same intercom system, so one can pick up the phone in Taipei and call the overseas offices on a direct line. Each employee has a direct phone extension with an individual employee number, and the telecommunication system is the same for intra-office transfers as it for inter-office calls. This is enormously convenient and enables efficient communication across the board.

What sets J. J. Pan and Partners apart from orthodox corporations is a focus on modesty and basic spiritual well-being. The firm holds a bi-monthly event to promote healthy activity outside the office environment. Friends and family also participate in these excursions. The March 2011 retreat envisioned a "Dialogue with Nature," and involved the entire firm hiking on the outskirts of Taipei, far away from the city's traffic congestion and environmental pollution.

The firm also provides educational opportunities for employees. Seminars run throughout the year to encourage employees to share information with each other as well as improve their personal knowledge. The multidisciplinary seminars take advantage of every department's expertise, with external instructors only hired as a last resort. This ensures that the topic of the seminar is completely relevant to the daily operations of the firm. All information from these educational sessions is consolidated and stored on a central server that can be accessed by all employees. The most current issues covered include sustainability, including architectural case studies; urban design concepts and realizations; design software integration; new technologies and details, and specific design strategies.

The firm provides lunch daily for employees in the canteen, a service very few companies still provide, but just one of the things that makes J. J. Pan and Partners unique and reflects its holistic approach to employee welfare. The lunch breaks are in two one-hour shifts with a half-hour overlap; the first group eats at 12:00 and rests from 12:30 to 1:00 while the second group eats at 12:30 and rests from 1:00 to 1:30. The shifts change monthly to offer more variety and flexibility between departments and, more importantly, serve as bonding time in an already close-knit office.

Organic growth does not happen without constant self-evaluation and calculated improvements. Like many architectural firms, J. J. Pan and Partners is looking to integrate Revit into the office, but there are many aspects at play beyond just fluency with the program. Implementing Revit will also change the personnel makeup and structure of the firm. The traditional AutoCAD firm consists of a smaller design team and a bigger post-design team to produce the CD and perform cost analysis and material schedules. A Revit-based firm requires a larger design team to set up and initiate projects with the complex program, which essentially displaces much of the post-design team as Revit handles much of that responsibility as part of Building Information Modeling. Mr. Pan's goal is to carefully integrate the technology with small, familiar projects so that the firm can still practice responsibly and design effectively while negotiating the steep learning curve.

The environment at J. J. Pan and Partners is structured yet elastic, ordered yet congenial, with the management team diverse and professional; consequently, the office reflects these traits. The refreshing feature is the way the firm is able to incorporate a sociopetal atmosphere typical of small

companies as the basis for a large firm. The efficiency, quality and delivery of projects are not diminished; in fact, the atmosphere and office management style promotes output by establishing a truly healthy workplace. This prominent international firm may not be the model for glamour or extravagance, but its success and productivity is undeniable, its atmosphere unique and nurturing. It's no wonder employees all liken the firm to a big family, analogous to the humble residential units from which it stems.

Jack Kuo

Doctor of Architecture,
School of Architecture, University of Hawaii at Mānoa

Biographies

Joshua Jih Pan, FAIA
Founding Principal

Joshua Jih Pan completed his Bachelor of Science degree at National Cheng Kung University in Taiwan. He received his professional degree from Rice University in Houston, Texas in 1966 and won the AIA Henry Adams Award, Black-Brollier Scholarship, and the MN Davidson Award for Graduating Student in Architecture. In 1967 he earned his Master of Science in Architecture/Urban Design degree from Columbia University, New York City, where he was awarded a full-tuition scholarship and the William Kinne Fellows Traveling Fellowship.

Before returning to Taiwan in 1976, Pan worked at the firms of Philip Johnson & Richard Foster; Davis, Brody & Associates in New York; and Collins Uhl Hoisington Anderson in New Jersey. He obtained his US professional license in 1972, Taiwan license in 1977, and was awarded Class I registered architect status in China in the year 2009.

Pan founded J. J. Pan and Partners in 1981, and the firm has since won scores of awards for design excellence—locally and internationally—in addition to the numerous publications highlighting the firm's projects. Other than his professional work, Pan has taught periodically over the last 30 years as adjunct professor at Chung Yuan Christian University, the National Taipei Institute of Technology, Tunghai University, National Chiao Tung University and the National Taiwan University of Science and Technology. He was awarded the Honorary Professorship of Jiangnan University, China in 2009. Beyond academia, Pan also served as the president of the Chinese Institute of Urban Design and director of both the Taipei Architects' Association and the Architectural Institute of the Republic of China (ROC).

Pan was elected Fellow of the American Institute of Architects in 1994, and in 1996 received Taiwan's prestigious ROC Outstanding Architect Award from the national government for lifetime achievement. In 1998, Commonwealth magazine listed Pan as one of the 200 personalities most influential in shaping Taiwan's future development. He frequently serves as a design juror and critic and is often invited to speak at domestic and international conferences.

Jason Chen
Principal

Jason Chen joined J. J. Pan and Partners in 1981 after earning his Master of Science in Architecture from National Cheng Kung University and Bachelor of Architecture from Chung Yuan Christian University, where he completed his thesis design under Professor Joshua J. Pan. After a 10-year absence for personal career development, he returned to the firm in 1999 and became a principal the following year, responsible for project execution, information management, quality control and the firm's operation while providing leadership for design teams.

While assuming the role of principal, Chen studied EMBA at National Chengchi University to acquire the solid foundations of management expertise. With his diverse educational background, he has been overseeing the firm's general management since 2007 while successfully leading the firm through the global financial crisis. Chen has also been instrumental in developing the firm's core competencies, promoting talent training, as well as implementing Knowledge Management to complement J. J. Pan and Partners' comprehensive design basis and promoting the firm's sustainable growth.

Jong-Yu Cheng
Principal

Jong-Yu Cheng joined J. J. Pan and Partners in 1982 after receiving his Bachelor of Architecture from Chung Yuan Christian University. Recognized for his design talents, Cheng has accumulated considerable professional experience across a broad range of building types— including institutional, commercial, residential, office and mixed-use development—while specializing in high-tech industrial projects. As a principal since 2000, his thorough understanding of clients' needs has seen him closely involved in a variety of projects. He is also responsible for overseeing the firm's active practice in China.

On top of his extensive professional experience gained through almost thirty years of practice, Cheng is currently pursuing an EMBA at National Taiwan University to further his management expertise. His artistic sketches, noted for their simple line work conveying evocative imagery, were well received while exhibited in "Sketch Up! Exhibition of Taiwanese Contemporary Architects' Sketches."

Chung-Tsai Huang
Principal

Chung-Tsai Huang joined J. J. Pan and Partners in 1987, assuming the positions of cost estimation manager, vice president of construction administration and executive vice president. In these roles, he oversees the firm's overall development, coordination between design and construction supervision departments and project management to produce functionally and financially feasible projects within the professional quality standards. Since 2005, after being elected as a principal, he has contributed significantly to the firm's commissions in all phases of project management from inception to completion.

Huang is a graduate of Feng Chia University, where he obtained his Bachelor of Civil Engineering. Recognized for his invaluable experience in management and construction, he is an adjunct assistant professor at the Graduate Institute of Architecture, National Chiao Tung University; an adjunct instructor at the Department of Architecture, Huafan University; and a frequent lecturer at various architecture-related conferences.

Chungwei Su
Principal

Chungwei Su joined J. J. Pan and Partners in 1991 after studying and working in the US. He has extensive experience in multinational design collaborations with renowned practices in the US, Japan, Germany, Holland and China. He was named as a principal in 2004, contributing his knowledge of international practice as well as his active involvement in numerous projects of grand scale and design significance.

Su received his Master of Architecture in Urban Design from Harvard University Graduate School of Design and Bachelor of Architecture from Chung Yuan Christian University. While committed to creative design in the professional field, he has also been continually sharing his knowledge and thinking through teaching and lecturing at institutions for architectural education, including National Chiao Tung University, National Taiwan University of Science and Technology, Chung Yuan Christian University, as well as leading academic forums in architects' associations. In recognition of his outstanding professional and academic achievement, he received the Architectural Gold Medal from the Ministry of the Interior in 1994, an Architectural Design Excellence Award in 1995, and was named Taiwan's ROC Outstanding Architect in 2007. He is a registered architect in Taiwan, China and the US.

Rocky Huang
Principal

General Manager, Horizon
Design Shanghai Office

Since joining J. J. Pan and Partners in 1987, Rocky Huang has brought to the firm extensive experience in a wide variety of large scale high-tech projects. In recognition of his expertise, he was appointed general manager of Horizon Design Shanghai Office in 2003, in charge of business development, client relationships as well as management of regional business in China. He was appointed a principal of the firm in 2005.

Huang graduated in Civil Engineering from Lan Yang Institute of Technology in Taiwan and completed his EMBA at the reputable Fudan University in Shanghai. To share his valuable experience in management and construction, he has been committed to academia as a guest lecturer at Chung Hua University, National Chiao Tung University in Taiwan and Tongji University in Shanghai.

Robin C.K. Tang
Associate

General Manager, Horizon
Design Xiamen Office

Robin Tang joined J. J. Pan and Partners in 1994, promoted through the positions of designer, project architect, project manager and associate of the design department. He has led design teams for projects in Taipei, Shanghai, Beijing, Xiamen and Shenzhen. In view of his comprehensive performance in all disciplines, he has been head of Horizon Design Xiamen Office since 2006, responsible for various projects including residential, educational, commercial, industrial buildings and urban planning and design in southern China.

Tang graduated from Columbia University Graduate School of Architecture, Planning and Preservation where he received his Master of Science in Advanced Architectural Design with the Lucille Smyser Lowenfish Memorial Prize. He also studied in a National Taiwan University of Science and Technology EMBA program for executive courses.

Jen-Chieh Cheng
Associate

General Manager, Horizon
Design Tianjin Office

Since joining J. J. Pan and Partners in 2003, Jen-Chieh Cheng has been assigned as core team member of business expansion in China. In recognition of his outstanding design performance, he worked as lead designer, project manager and design director in the Horizon Design Shanghai Office, where he contributed to projects through all phases of development. The breadth of his expertise is remarkable in all aspects, from ingenuity in complex projects, to project development and corporate management. For his solid experience, he was relocated to Tianjin in 2006 to extend the firm's business to another strategic development hub in north China.

Cheng obtained his Master of Architecture from National Taiwan University of Science and Technology. With his in-depth knowledge and extensive experience, he actively participates in both professional and academic events in China representing the firm's younger generation of designers.

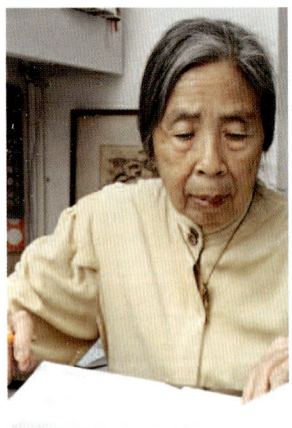

Chiu-Hwa Wang
Consulting Architect

Chiu-Hwa Wang received her Bachelor of Science in Architecture from the National Central University in China, and her degree of Master of Science in Architecture from Columbia University in New York. From 1953–79 she worked in collaboration with Percival Goodman, FAIA, first as designer, then associate, and finally partner. In 1979 Ms Wang moved to Taiwan, where she taught at the Taipei Institute of Technology and Tamkang University, while also serving as architectural consultant to a number of public institutions.

In 1983, after winning a design competition for the main library of Chung Yuan Christian University in collaboration with Joshua J. Pan, she started her own professional practice and has since been working in joint venture with J. J. Pan and Partners on a number of projects. Recognized for her academic and professional achievements, she was named Outstanding Architect of Taiwan ROC in 2003.

Associates

Kao-Hsin Chang

Chih-Ming Chang

Hsiao-Ming Chang

Chia-Yun Chen

Kuen-Feng Chen

Shao-Ping Chen

Steven B.J. Chen

Jen-Chieh Cheng

Shun-Yi Cheng

Grace C.M. Heh

Pin-I Hou

Steve Kuo Hsu

Genie Huang

Mitcheal C.S. Huang

Raymond R.M. Huang

Yung-Bin Huang

Hung-Ta Hung

Chun-Sheng Lee

Pen Lee

Frank C.C. Liao

Chi-Hsun Liao

Simon Y.T. Lin

Ling Pan

Oui Ming Sae-Tang

Ching-Feng Shen

Yi-Chyau Su

Robin C.K. Tang

Ady H.S. Tsai

Chih-Wei Tsai

Tzuu-Lieh Tsai

Henry W. Y. Yen

Chiu-Ping Wang

Fang-Cheng Wu

Awards and Honors

2010   Public Construction Golden Quality Award for Architecture
Kinman County Datung Home

2009   Excellence in Innovative High-tech Construction Award, Science Park
TSMC Fab 12 Phase 4, Connection Bridge

Jiangxi Outstanding Architecture Design Award, 2nd place
Nanchang Factory Plant

Quality Award, FIABCI-Taiwan Real Estate Excellence Award
Scientific Research Building, Feng Chia University

2008   Gold Plaque Award, Taoyuan Architecture Award for Industrial/Commercial Building
Test Research Inc. (TRI) Headquarters

Taiwan Interior Design Award of Working Space
Kingyorker Headquarters

AIA New York State Award of Excellence for Adaptive Reuse
Horizon Design Shanghai Office

Best Historic Preservation Project, The 2nd Biannual Business Week/Architectural Record China Awards
Horizon Design Shanghai Office

2006   Citation, *TAIWAN ARCHITECT* Annual Design Award
Scooter Garage, National Chiao Tung University

Silver Plaque Award, Taipei City New Look Award for Open Space
Taipei Truth Lutheran Church

AIA New York State Citation Award
Taipei Truth Lutheran Church

Shanghai Outstanding Residential Project Award, Monomial Design, 3rd place
Greenland Shanghai Plaza

2005   World Association of Chinese Architects Gold Medal Award
Scooter Garage, National Chiao Tung University

Silver Plaque Award, Taoyuan Architecture Award for Housing
Acer Long Term Residential Development III

Silver Plaque Award, Taoyuan Architecture Award for Industrial Building
Quanta TFT/LCD Plant

2004   Public Construction Golden Quality Award for Architectural Design
Szu Zhih New Town

2003   China Service Apartment Design Prize, 2nd place
Greenland Shanghai Plaza

2001   AIA New York Chapter Annual Design Award
Da-Sha House, Chinese Culture University

National Building Design Award for Intelligent Building
Macronix Headquarters Building

1999	Renowned Finalist, Far Eastern Outstanding Architects Design Award
	Founder's Memorial Library, Chinese Culture University
	Quality Excellence Award, National Public Construction Annual Award
	National Museum of Marine Biology/Aquarium
1998	Taiwan Provincial Building Design Award
	Engineering Building, Chung Yuan Christian University
1997	National Building Design Award for Passive Energy Efficiency
	Library, Chung Yuan Christian University
	Architecture Golden Award of R.O.C.
	My House Cherry Grove Housing
1995	Taiwan Provincial Building Design Award
	Student Center, National Chiao Tung University
	Architecture Golden Award of R.O.C.
	Synpac Sunshine State Housing
1994	Citation, *CHINESE ARCHITECT* Annual Design Award
	Main Library & Information Sciences Center, National Chung Cheng University
1993	Silver Plaque Award, *CHINESE ARCHITECT* Annual Design Award
	Sung Chiang Poetry Park
	Taiwan Provincial Building Design Award
	Main Library, National Changhua University of Education
1992	Silver Plaque Award, *CHINESE ARCHITECT* Annual Design Award
	Gymnasium and Indoor Swimming Pool, Chung Yuan Christian University
1991	National Building Design Award for Passive Energy Efficiency
	Precision Instrument Development Center for the National Science Council
	Citation, *CHINESE ARCHITECT* Annual Design Award
	Medical Research Building & Conference Center, Taichung Veterans General Hospital
1990	Taiwan Provincial Building Design Award
	Medical Research Building & Conference Center, Taichung Veterans General Hospital
1989	Taipei Municipal Building Design Award
	Overseas Radio and Television New Office
1988	Taiwan Provincial Building Design Award
	Library, Chung Yuan Christian University
	Ten Most Outstanding 'Creativity in Architecture' Award
	Gymnasium, National Taiwan Ocean University
1985	Gold Plaque Award, *CHINESE ARCHITECT* Annual Design Award
	Library, Chung Yuan Christian University

Chronological List of Selected Buildings and Projects

1981–94
Multiple-Stage Renewal,
National Taiwan Ocean University,
Keelung, Taiwan

1984
China Wheat Products
Research & Development Institute,
Taipei

★● 1985
Library, Chung Yuan Christian University,
Taoyuan, Taiwan

● 1989
Main Library, National Taiwan Ocean
University, Keelung, Taiwan

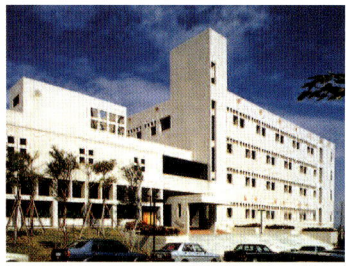

★● 1989
Medical Research Building & Conference
Center, Taichung Veterans General Hospital,
Taichung, Taiwan

★ 1991
Sung Chiang Poetry Park,
Taipei

★● 1991
Indoor Swimming Pool,
Chung Yuan Christian University,
Taoyuan, Taiwan

★ 1992
Student Center,
National Chiao Tung University,
Hsinchu, Taiwan

1992
Winbond IC Wafer Fab II,
Hsinchu Science Park, Taiwan

1993

Information Science & Electrical Engineering Building, National Tsing Hua University, Hsinchu, Taiwan

★● 1993

Main Library & Information Sciences Center, National Chung Cheng University, Chiayi, Taiwan

1994

Yung Ho Church, Taipei

1995

Research & Development Center, Development Center for Biotechnology, Taipei

★ 1996

My House Cherry Grove Housing, Taipei

1996

TSMC Fab 3 & 4, Hsinchu Science Park, Taiwan

★ 1996

Synpac Sunshine State Housing, Taoyuan, Taiwan

1997

Grace Gospel Center, MonEng Presbyterian Church, Taichung, Taiwan

1998

Etron Headquarters Building, Hsinchu Science Park, Taiwan

★ Award/Honor
● Joint venture with C. H. Wang Architect
■ Competition entry/Unbuilt

★● 1998
Founder's Memorial Library,
Chinese Culture University,
Taipei

★ 1999
Acer Long Term Residential Development III,
Taoyuan, Taiwan

1999
Primax Headquarters Building,
Hsinchu Science Park, Taiwan

★ 1999
Macronix Headquarters Building,
Hsinchu Science Park, Taiwan

★● 1999
Da-Sha House,
Chinese Culture University,
Taipei

2000
Standard Factory Phase I,
Hsinchu Science Park, Taiwan

2001
Administration Building, Nan Kai College,
Nanto, Taiwan

★ 2001
Quanta TFT/LCD Plant,
Taoyuan, Taiwan

2002
Winbond Technology Building,
Taipei

2003
Macronix Recreation/Training Center,
Hsinchu Science Park. Taiwan

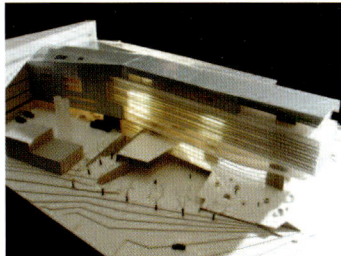

■ 2003
Quanta R&D Center Project,
Taipei

2003
TSMC Fab 12 & Headquarters,
Hsinchu Science Park, Taiwan

2003–08
Suang-Lien Social Welfare Park,
Taipei

2004
ASUSTeK Headquarters Complex,
Taipei

2004
BJSC Fab IV & V,
Beijing, China

★ 2004
Scooter Garage,
National Chiao Tung University,
Hsinchu, Taiwan

2004
Holistic Education Village,
Chung Yuan Christian University,
Taoyuan, Taiwan

2004
Kingland Mansion,
Shanghai, China

★ Award/Honor
● Joint venture with C. H. Wang Architect
■ Competition entry/Unbuilt

2004
ZyXEL R&D Campus,
Jiangsu, China

★ 2004
Taipei Truth Lutheran Church,
Taipei

2005
Aero Science Building,
Feng Chia University,
Taichung, Taiwan

2005
MediaTek Headquarters,
Hsinchu Science Park, Taiwan

★ 2005
Shanghai Greenland Plaza,
Shanghai, China

★ 2005
Horizon Design Shanghai Office,
Shanghai, China

● 2005
Gymnasium, Chinese Culture University,
Taipei

2006
Research Building, College of Medicine,
Fu Jen Catholic University,
Taipei

2007
Fleur de Chine Hotel,
Sun Moon Lake,
Nanto, Taiwan

2007

Taipei Street Furniture Design,
Taipei

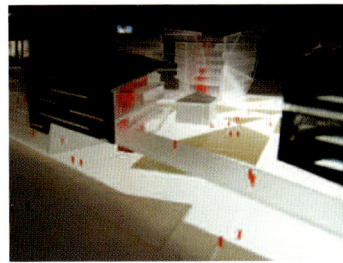

■ 2007

Ningbo Industrial Design & Creative Center
Project, Zhejiang, China

2007

VIA Shenzhen R&D Center,
Guangdong, China

2007

ZyXEL Recreation Center,
Hsinchu Science Park, Taiwan

2008

Xue Si Building, Feng Chia University,
Taichung, Taiwan

2008

Kingland Ningbo Financial Center,
Zhejiang, China

2008

Kingyorker Headquarters,
Taipei

2008

Test Research Inc. Headquarters,
Taoyuan, Taiwan

2009

School Buildings, Ginling Girls' High School,
Taipei

★ Award/Honor
● Joint venture with C. H. Wang Architect
■ Competition entry/Unbuilt

2009

Huga Fab III and Headquarters Building,
Central Taiwan Science Park, Taiwan

■ 2009

Taiwan Dramatic Arts Center Project,
Taipei

2009

IMPAX Lab Taiwan Plant Phase I,
Chunan Science Park, Taiwan

2009

Lien Hwa Headquarters,
Taipei

★ 2009

Nanchang Factory Plant,
Jiangxi, China

2009

Pegatron Shanghai Campus,
Shanghai, China

2009

Church of Suang-Lien Center for the Elderly,
Taipei

2009

Standard Factory Phase II,
Pingtung Agricultural Biotechnology Park,
Taiwan

2009

Neo Solar Power Office Building Complex,
Hsinchu Science Park, Taiwan

★ 2009
TSMC Fab12 Phase 4,
Hsinchu Science Park, Taiwan

2011
National Taichung Digital Library,
Taichung, Taiwan

2011
Rutgers Community Christian Church,
New Jersey, USA

2011
Hunya Chocolate Museum,
Taipei

2012
Sanya Tropical Resort Hotel,
Hainan, China

2012
Phase II Construction, Fuzhou Vocational
and Technical Institute, Fujian, China

2012
Research Headquarters,
National Chengchi University,
Taipei

2012
Cancer/Proton Center,
National Taiwan University Hospital,
Taipei

2013
Flagship Building,
Huashan Cultural Creative Center,
Taipei

★ Award/Honor
● Joint venture with C. H. Wang Architect
■ Competition entry/Unbuilt

Project Credits

Horizon Design Shanghai Office

Principal-In-Charge: Joshua Jih Pan, Rocky Huang

Design Team: Jong-Yu Cheng, Yu-Ting Wu, Jen-Chieh Cheng, Ady H.S. Tsai, Jason C.L. Wu, Li-Kai Lee, Yu-Lin Lee

Client: Horizon Design Co., Ltd.(Shanghai)

Structural Consultant: Team Engineering Consulting Ltd.; Shanghai Long Heng Decoration Co., Ltd.

MEP Consultant: Shanghai JinRi M&E Installing Co., Ltd

General Contractor: Shanghai Long Heng Decoration Co., Ltd.

Photographer: Jim Chang, Steve Mok, Heng Zhong Lu, J. J. Pan and Partners

ZyXEL R & D Campus

Principal-In-Charge: Jong-Yu Cheng

Design Team: Rocky Huang, Ady H.S. Tsai, Pin-I Hou, Martin Hagel, Shigetaka Ito, Pen Lee, Mallet Y.L. Chang, Hsiao-Mei Shih, Han-Yi Chu

Client: ZyXEL Communications Corp.

Structural Consultant: Team Engineering Consulting Ltd.; Jing Ding Engineering & Construction Co., Ltd.; Jiangsu Nongken Architectural Design Institute

MEP Consultant: Jing Ding Engineering & Construction Co., Ltd.; Jiangsu Nongken Architectural Design Institute

Landscape: Horizon Design Co., Ltd.(Shanghai)

Interior: Horizon Design Co., Ltd.(Shanghai)

General Contractor: Jiangsu Wentong Construction Co., Ltd.

Photographer: Jim Cheng, Heng-Zhong Lu

Kingyorker Headquarters

Principal-In-Charge: Chungwei Su

Design Team: Ming-Yuan Wang, Rax Y.S. Huang, Ady H.S. Tsai, Shiao-Mei Shih, Joseph J.Y. Chou, Kai-Ping Fang, Kao-Ming Yang

Client: Kingyorker Enterprise Co., Ltd.

Structural Consultant: Team Engineering Consulting Ltd.

MEP Consultant: C.H. Wu Consulting Engineers

Landscape: J. J. Pan and Partners

Interior: JAHAA Design

General Contractor: Shen Cheng Construction Co., Ltd.

BRB pattern: National Center for Research on Earthquake Engineering

Photographer: JAHAA Design, J. J. Pan and Partners

Taipei Street Furniture Design

Principal-In-Charge: Joshua Jih Pan

Design Team: Chungwei Su, Steven B.J. Chen, Ming-Yuan Wang, Kevin B.I. Yu, Yen-Chih Tseng, Jien-Yu Chen, Hsuan-Ming Wu, Kao-Ming Yang

Client: Omniad Media Incorporation

Structural Consultant: Team Engineering Consulting Ltd.

Photographer: J. J. Pan and Partners

TSMC Fab12, Phase 4

Principal-In-Charge: Joshua Jih Pan

Design Team: Jong-Yu Cheng, Chih-Wei Tsai, Steven B.J. Chen, Liang-Chen Hung, Chien-Hung Shen, Shun-Lang Wu, Kun-Chou Lin, Shu-Chiao Hsu, Kuan-Ju Hou, Chun-Kai Shih, Shih-Fang Huang, Yeng-Bin Huang, Yi-Chyau Su, Hung-Ta Hung, Wei-Fu Shih, Shun-I Yu, Yi-Sung Liu, Cheng-Hon Su, Kuang-Wu Hou, Kuo-Hao Hsu, Meng-Chieh Chen, Yung-Ching Pan

Client: Taiwan Semiconductor Manufacturing Company

Structural Consultant: Team Engineering Consulting Ltd.

Water & Soil Conservation: Chung Chi Technical Consultant Co., Ltd.

General Contractor: Fu Tsu Construction Co., Ltd.; Tasa Construction Corp.

Photographer: David Chen

Test Research Inc. (TRI) Headquarters

Principal-In-Charge: Joshua Jih Pan

Design Team: Yi-Tai Lin, Borden Tseng, Chien-Hung Shen, Shih-Fang Huang, I-Fen Chang, Kuan-Ju Hou, Hung-Ta Hung, Li-Kai Lee, Fang-Cheng Wu

Client: Test Research, Inc.

Structural Consultant: Team Engineering Consulting Ltd.

MEP Consultant: Arnold Consulting Engineers Service; Yuan Tai Engineering Consulting Co., Ltd.

Landscape: J. J. Pan and Partners

Interior: Horizon Design Co., Ltd.

General Contractor: Chung-Lin General Contractors, Ltd.

Photography: J. J. Pan and Partners

Dingpu MRT Station

Principal-In-Charge: Chungwei Su

Design Team: Chun-Yi Lee, Chi-Hsiang Chen, Kuan-Ju Hou, Fu-Tse Tang, Chia-Cheng Wei, Wei-Luen Huang, Tien-Kai Yang, Tzu-Hua Wu

Client: Department of Rapid Transit Systems, Taipei City Government

Structural Consultant: Moh and Associates, Inc. (platform and track); Envision Engineering Consultants (entrance); K.C. Structure Engineering Office (entrance and basement of joint development building)

MEP Consultant: Moh and Associates, Inc.

Landscape: J. J. Pan and Partners

Architectural Façade System Consultant: Lead Dao Technology & Engineering Ltd. (entrance construction)

Geo-tech Consultant: Moh and Associates, Inc.

General Contractor: Chuan Yuan Construction Co., Ltd.; Iwata Chizaki Construction Corporation

Sanya Tropical Resort Hotel

Principal-In-Charge: Joshua Jih Pan

Design Team: Jong-Yu Cheng, Pan Lin, Yen-Chie Tseng, Bo-Yang Lin, Zai-Wen Huang; Hainan Yuanzheng Architectural Design and Consultation Co., Ltd.

Client: San Ya Bao Kang Tourism Co., Ltd.

Structural Consultant: Team Engineering Consulting Ltd.
Shenzhen International Impression Architecture Designing Co., Ltd.

MEP Consultant: Hainan Yuanzheng Architectural Design and Consultation Co., Ltd.

Landscape: COSMOS Inc., Planning and Design Consultants

Lighting: Brandston Partnership Inc.

Interior: JAHAA Design

MediaTek Headquarters

Principal-In-Charge: Joshua Jih Pan, Jason Chen

Design Team: Steven B. J. Chen, Ming-Yuan Wang, Shun-Lang Wu, Liang-Chen Hung, I-Li Mao, Chun-Yi Lee, Shun-I Yu, Tai-An Lu

Client: MediaTek Inc.

Structural Engineer: Team Engineering Consulting Ltd.

MEP Consultant: I. S. Lin Associates Consulting Engineers; Idee Engineering Consulting Co., Ltd.

Landscape: Environmental Arts Design

Lighting: Chroma33 Architectural Lighting Design Inc.

General Contractor: Fu Tsu Construction Co., Ltd.

Photographer: Jeffrey Chang

Lien Hwa Headquarters

Principal-In-Charge: Joshua Jih Pan

Design Team: Chungwei Su, Ming-Yuan Wang, Ady H.S. Tsai, Kao-Hsin Chang, Hsueh-Fen Chien, Hsuan-Ming Wu, I-Hsuan Hsieh, Shih-Fang Huang, Yen-Chieh Lee, Tzuu-Lieh Tsai, Kuo-Long Tsao

Client: Lien Hwa Industrial Corp.

Structural Consultant: Team Engineering Consulting Ltd.

MEP Consultant: C.H. Wu Consulting Engineers

Landscape: Innerscapes Design

Lighting: Chroma33 Architectural Lighting Design Inc.

General Contractor: Sun Pao Tsun Construction Co., Ltd.

Photographer: Jeffrey Chang, Kevin Wu, J. J. Pan and Partners

Pegatron Shanghai Campus

Principal-In-Charge: Jong-Yu Cheng

Design Team: Martin Hagel, Pin-I Hou, Peter B.D. Wu, Chi-Han Lin; Pegatron (T.H. Tung, Alain Lee and Pegacasa)

Client: Pegatron (Shanghai) Technology Co., Ltd.

Structural Consultant: H.Y. International Architects Co., Ltd.

MEP Consultant: Kun Shan Yun-Ding Engineering Corp.

Landscape: J. J. Pan and Partners; Smart Style Landscape Consulting Co., Ltd.

Lighting: J. J. Pan and Partners

Interior: J. J. Pan and Partners; Pegatron (T.H. Tung, Alain Lee and Pegacasa)

General Contractor: Shanghai Tokeneso Construction Co., Ltd.

Photographer: John Wang, J. J. Pan and Partners

Gymnasium, Chinese Culture University

Principal-In-Charge: Joshua Jih Pan

Joint Venture Architect: Chiu-Hwa Wang

Design Team: Oui Ming Sae-Tang, Ann Y.H. Cheng, Ming-Yuan Wang, Ady H.S. Tsai, Kao-Hsing Chang, Kevin F. Hsieh, Kevin B.Y. Yu, Yen-Lin Huang, Rax Y.S. Huang, Mallet Y.L. Chang, Shu-Hui Lin, Pei-Shih Chou, Wei-Xi Chang, Joseph J.Y. Chen, Lisa Y.H. Chen, Tien-Kai Yang, Yen-Chieh Lee, Chu-Bin Wang, Tzuu-Lieh Tsai, Jian-Hua Chen, Kevin C.R. Yang, Kuang-Chi Huang, Shun-I Yu

Client: Chinese Culture University

Structural Consultant/sketch: King-Le Chang and Associates

MEP Consultant: Elite Consultant Engineers & Associates; I. S. Lin Associates Consulting Engineers

Water & Soil Conservation: San Ya Engineering Consultant

Geo-tech Consultant: Chung Chi Technical Consultant Co., Ltd.

Acoustic Consultant: Professor Wei-Hwa Chiang, Ph.D.

Landscape: Environmental Arts Design

Lighting: Chroma33 Architectural Lighting Design Inc.

Interior: J. J. Pan and Partners/C.H. Wang Architect

General Contractor: Chuan Yuan Construction Co., Ltd.

Photographer: Marc Gerritsen, Jeffrey Chang, Webber Huang

ZyXEL Recreation Center

Principal-In-Charge: Joshua Jih Pan, Chungwei Su

Design Team: Chia-Lin Liu, Shigetaka Ito, Ming-Yuan Wang, Chien-Hung Shen, Tsung-Yin Lee, Cheng-Yin Tsai, Yi-Chyau Su

Client: ZyXEL Communications Corp.

Structural Consultant: Team Engineering Consulting Ltd.

MEP Consultant: C.H. Wu Consulting Engineers

Landscape: J. J. Pan and Partners

Interior: J. J. Pan and Partners

General Contractor: Fu Tai Construction Co., Ltd.

Photographer: J. J. Pan and Partners

Fleur de Chine Hotel, Sun Moon Lake

Principal-In-Charge: Joshua Jih Pan

Design Team: Jong Yu Cheng, Chung-Tsai Huang , Shao-Ping Chen, Martin Hagel, Ming-Yuan Wang, Shih-Cheng Yang, Yi-Shien Chin, David J.H. Wu, Wen-Yang Chen

Client: L'Hotel de Chine Group

Structural Consultant: Team Engineering Consulting Ltd.

MEP Consultant: New Plan Electrical & Mechanical Engineers

Landscape: Ecoscape Formosana

Lighting: Chroma33 Architectural Lighting Design Inc.

Interior: Wu's Deco Design Co., Ltd.

General Contractor: Gu He Construction Co., Ltd.

Photographer: J. J. Pan and Partners

Neo Solar Power Office Building Complex

Principal-In-Charge: Joshua Jih Pan

Design Team: Chungwei Su, Chung-Tsai Huang, Yi-Tai Lin, Martin Hagel, Shun-Lang Wu, Mallet Y.L. Chang, Kun-Chao Lin, I-Fen Chang, Shu-Chiao Hsu, Chiu-Ping Wang, Chieh-Hui Wu

Client: Neo Solar Power Corporation

Structural Consultant: Team Engineering Consulting Ltd.

Mechanical Consultant: Home Run Electrical Engineers Associates

General Contractor: Fu Tsu Construction Co., Ltd.; Lead Fu Industrials Corp.

Photographer: Jeffrey Cheng

Huga Fab III and Headquarters Building

Principal-In-Charge: Jason Chen

Design Team: Shun-Yi Cheng, Martin Hagel, May Su, Yi-Shien Chin, Shih-Cheng Yang, Wen-Chi Wang, Shih-Fang Huang, Yi-Chyau Su, Chun-Sheng Lee, Chin-Chiu Chiu

Client: Huga Optotech Inc.

Structural Consultant: Team Engineering Consulting Ltd.

MEP Consultant: Marketech International Corp.

Interior: Horizon Design Co., Ltd. (3rd and 4th Floor)

General Contractor: Fu Tsu Construction Co., Ltd.

Photographer: Chun Chieh Liu

IMPAX Lab Taiwan Plant Phase I

Principal-In-Charge: Joshua Jih Pan

Design Team: Oui Ming Sae-Tang, Pen Lee, Li-Jiun Lu, Johnnie J.S. Kuo, Ming-Huang Tsai, Shun-I Yu, Chiu-Ping Wang, Yi-Chyau Su

Client: Impax Laboratories(Taiwan) Ltd.

Structural Consultant: Team Engineering Consulting Ltd.

MEP Consultant: Fu-Tai Engineering Co. Ltd.

Landscape: J. J. Pan and Partners

Interior: J. J. Pan and Partners, Horizon Design Co., Ltd.

General Contractor: Fu Tsu Construction Co., Ltd.

Photographer: Jeffrey Cheng, Kevin Wu, J. J. Pan and Partners

Church of Suang-Lien Center for the Elderly

Principal-In-Charge: Joshua Jih Pan

Design Team: Chung-Tsai Huang, Steven B.J. Chen, Wei-Shih Hsieh, Chiao-Yuan Wu, Pen Lee, Yi-Sung Liu, Tzuu-Lieh Tsai, Kuo-Long Tsao

Client: Taiwan Presbyterian Suang-Lien Church

Structural Consultant: Team Engineering Consulting Ltd.

MEP Consultant: C.H. Wu Consulting Engineers

Lighting: Ming-Yu Hsu

Architectural Façade System Consultant: Lead Dao Technology & Engineering Ltd.

Interior: J. J. Pan and Partners

General Contractor: Gin Zon Construction Co., Ltd.; Yuan Den Engineering Co., Ltd.

Photographer: David Chen, Yi-Wen Chen, Wei-Shih Hsieh, J. J. Pan and Partners

Taoyuan International Airport Access MRT Stations

Principal-In-Charge: Joshua Jih Pan, Chungwei Su

Design Team: Chia-Lin Liu, Fu-Chi Tang, Rui-Heng Lu, Song-Ju Chen, Chi-Yuen Chiang, Shun-Yi Cheng, David B.D. Wu, Wei-Ken Kuo, Kevin C.K. Lin, Chien-Yuan Liang, Chia-Wei Ting, Chien-Yu Chen, Tzu-Hua Wu, San-Min Lee, Hui-Ju Dai

Client: Bureau of High Speed Rail, Ministry of Transportation and Communications

Structural Consultant: CECI Engineering Consultants, Inc., Taiwan (platform and track); Team Engineering Consulting Ltd. (upper structure)

MEP Consultant: CECI Engineering Consultants, Inc., Taiwan

Landscape: J. J. Pan and Partners

Lighting: J. J. Pan and Partners

Interior: J. J. Pan and Partners

Architectural Façade System Consultant: Lead Dao Technology & Engineering Ltd. (A2 station connection bridge)

Geo-tech Consultant: CECI Engineering Consultants, Inc., Taiwan

General Contractor: Da Cin Construction Co., Ltd. ; Hwang Chang General Contractor Co., Ltd.

Research Building, College of Medicine at Fu Jen Catholic University

Principal-In-Charge: Joshua Jih Pan

Design Team: Mitchell C.S. Huang, Ho-Ping Chueh, Ming-Yuan Wang, Steven B.J. Chen, Shu-Ching Wu, Chun-Yi Lee, Shu-Huei Lin, Jie-Ling Lu, Yin-Chuan Ho, Yi-Chyau Su

Client: Fu Jen Catholic University

Structural Consultant: King-Le Chang and Associates

MEP Consultant: Teddy Associates Consultant Ltd.; Yuan Tai Engineering Consulting Co., Ltd.

Waste water treatment: Rizing Sun Environmental Engineering Firm

General Contractor: Cheng Long Construction Co., Ltd.

Photographer: Jeffrey Chang, Ming-Hsung Tseng

School Buildings, Ginling Girls' High School

Principal-In-Charge: Joshua Jih Pan, Jason Chen
Design Team: Jason Chen, Wei-Ken Kuo, Wen-Chi Wang, Shao-Ping Chen, Mitchell C.S. Huang, Yi-Shien Chin, Shih-Cheng Yang, Bo-Hong Chen, Yuan-Pin Weng, Shih-Fang Huang, Cheng-Hwa Wu, Kuang-Chi Huang, Tzuu-Lieh Tsai
Client: Ginling Girls' High School
Structural Consultant: Team Engineering Consulting Ltd.
MEP Consultant: C.H. Wu Consulting Engineers
Landscape: J. J. Pan and Partners
Interior: J. J. Pan and Partners
General Contractor: Chuan Yuan Construction Co., Ltd.; Swun's Corporation
Photographer: David Chen

Research Headquarters, National Chengchi University

Principal-In-Charge: Joshua Jih Pan, Jason Chen
Design Team: Shao-Ping Chen, Mitchell C.S. Huang, Yi-Shien Chin, Yuan-Pin Weng, Sheng-Ping Lin, Chun-Hwa Liao
Client: National Chengchi University
Structural Consultant: Team Engineering Consulting Ltd.
MEP Consultant: C.H. Wu Consulting Engineers
Landscape: J. J. Pan and Partners
Interior: J. J. Pan and Partners

Ningbo Industrial Design & Creative Center

Principal-In-Charge: Joshua Jih Pan
Design Team: Jong-Yu Cheng, Pen Lee, Chia-Fang Chan, Yen-Chih Tseng, Chien-Yuan Liang, Chi-Wei Chen
Client: Ningbo Industrial Design Investment Development Co., Ltd.

Stockholm Library

Principal-In-Charge: Joshua Jih Pan
Design Team: Borden Tseng
Client: Stockholm City Council

HTC R & D Project

Principal-In-Charge: Chungwei Su, Jong-Yu Cheng
Design Team: Pen Lee, Chia-Fang Chan, Chien-Yuan Liang
Client: HTC Corporation

Quanta Display Inc. (QDI) R & D Center Project

Principal-In-Charge: Joshua Jih Pan
Design Team: Martin Hagel, Pin-I Hou, Yi-Tai Lin, Yen-Chih Tseng, Chien-Yuan Liang
Client: Quanta Display Inc.
Structural Consultant: King-Le Chang and Associates

Taiwan Dramatic Arts Center Project

Principal-In-Charge: Joshua Jih Pan
Design Team: Mitchell C.S. Huang, Mallet Y.L. Chang, Bo-Yang Lin, Shih-Wei Liang, Angel Hsiao
Client: Preparatory Office of the National Center of Heritage in Arts
Calligrapher: Yang-tze Tong
Theater Design consultant: Austin Wang
Acoustical consultant: Professor Wei-Hwa Chiang, Ph.D.

Flagship Building, Huashan Cultural Creative Center

Principal-In-Charge (competition stage): Joshua Jih Pan
Design Team: Chungwei Su, Steven B.J. Chen, Pen Lee, Bo-Yang Lin, Yen-Chih Tseng, Tieng-Yi Pan
Client: Taiwan Cultural-Creative Development Co., Ltd.
Calligrapher: Yang-tze Tong
Structural: King-Le Chang and Associates
Lighting: Min-Yu Hsu

National Taichung Digital Library

Principal-In-Charge: Joshua Jih Pan, Jason Chen
Design Team: Chi-Ming Chang, Sheng-Tien Yeh, Shang-Ping Lin, Wen-Chi Wang, Chien-Yuan Liang, Chi-Hsuan Peng, Han-Shen Chen, Tien-Yi Pan, Chia-Zhong Hsieh, Hsiao-Mei Shih, Wu-Ting Wu, Tien Kai Yang, Shih-Fan Huang, Chun-Long Liu, Cong-Sian Chen, Sung-Po Chen, Jen-Chieh Yi, Chun-Sheng Lee, Cyu-Jing Chen, Chi-Jen Liu, Hui-Chi Chen, Chung-Pig Yeh, Cheng-En Wang, Cheng-Chih Kao, Shang-Yi Tsai
Client: National Taichung Library
Structural Consultant: Team Engineering Consulting Ltd.
MEP Consultant: Sine & Associates M/ELEC, Consultants & Engineers
Lighting: J. J. Pan and Partners, Chroma33 Architectural Lighting Design Inc.
Architectural Façade System Consultant: Lead Dao Technology & Engineering Ltd.
Landscape: J. J. Pan and Partners
Interior: J. J. Pan and Partners
Furniture Consultant: C. H. Wang, Architect
General Contractor: Kong Chou Construction Enterprise
Photographer: J. J. Pan and Partners

Acknowledgements

The publication of this monograph represents an enduring process no less than the realization of an actual building project in terms of the demands on creativity and extensive collaborations. It is the result of thousands of hours of meticulous craftsmanship along with constant refinement from all participants over the past four years. The projects published in this book were developed in the same collaborative fashion in our office and would not have been possible without the extraordinary contributions of our clients, consultants and colleagues of different expertise.

The principals of J. J. Pan and Partners would like to express their sincere gratitude to those whose tireless efforts contributed to the making of this book. In our Office: Genie C.N. Huang for envisioning the direction of the publication; Lu H. Cheng for her perseverance and thoroughness in tracking and consolidating all editorial material; Sara Y.S. Hung for her wonderful graphic design and page formatting; Andrew Hsu and Jason Yu as interns on Sara Hung's team; Rebecca C.L. Chen and Rie C.M. Huang for their works of translating and processing English texts; Jack Kuo, Joey Yeh and David Lee for editing English text, especially for Jack's contribution of his essay. Lastly, Ling Lin's distinguished critiques and Bo-Cheng Wang's eloquent script have added sophistication to the writing.

Professor Shi-wei Lo's essay, with his extraordinary insight and critique regarding J. J. Pan and Partners' work, lends significant credibility to this book.

Nancy Lin, of AECOM, for giving her visionary advice and editorial critiques, both professional and personal, through her long-time observance and interaction with J. J. Pan and Partners, and for her précis in the monograph's introduction.

Lastly, this book's completion is greatly indebted to Paul Latham, Alessina Brooks, Mark Cleary, Debbie Ball, Rod Gilbert, and the talented editorial and design team at The Images Publishing Group for their encouragement, tireless communication and professionalism.

Special thanks to:

- Calligraphy – Yang-tze Tong(Taiwan Drama Arts Center Project) , Joshua Jih Pan

- Coordination of publication – Chungwei Su

- Sketch – King-Le Chang(Gymnasium, Chinese Culture University), Joshua Jih Pan

- Photography by past and present J. J. Pan and Partners colleagues – Shao-Ping Chen, Steven B.J. Chen, Yi-Wen Chen, Martin Hagel, Pin-Yi Hou, Wei-Shih Hsieh, Pen Lee, Chien-Yuan Liang, Joshua Jih Pan, Chien-Hung Shen, Wei-Fu Shih, Yen-Chih Tseng, David J.H. Wu, Shun-Lang Wu, Yu-Ting Wu

- Photography in the chronology – David Chen, Jeffrey Chang, Jim Chang, Bor-Nian Lin, Gina Lin, Chun-Chieh Liu, Min-Hsiung Tseng, John Wang

Index

Office Locations

J. J. PAN AND PARTNERS, Architects and Planners

21, Alley 12, Lane 118, Ren Ai Rd.,
Sec. 3, Taipei 10657

Tel:+886-2-27012617
Fax:+886-2-27004489
Email: jjpp@jjpan.com
http://www.jjpan.com

HORIZON DESIGN (Shanghai)

Suite F, 16F, 138, Pudong Avenue,
Pudong New Area, Shanghai 200120, China

Tel:+86-21-58872932
Fax:+86-21-58872934
Email: jjpp@jjpan-sh.com

HORIZON DESIGN (Xiamen)

Suite 2811, 189, Xiahe Rd.,
Xiamen, Fujian 361003, China

Tel:+86-592-2227370~1
Fax:+86-592-2227372
Email: jjpp@jjpan-xm.com

HORIZON DESIGN (Tianjin)

Suite1505, 188, Jie-Fang N. Rd.,
Tianjin 300042, China

Tel:+86-22-58299658
Fax:+86-22-23037518
Email: jjpp@jjpan-tj.com

HORIZON DESIGN Company Limited

3F, 178, Xinyi Road,
Sec. 3, Taipei 10658

Tel:+886-2-27077121
Fax:+886-2-27011858
Email: hdcl@hdcl.com.tw
http://www.hdcl.com.tw

TEAM Engineering Consulting Limited

10, Alley 12, Lane 118, Ren Ai Rd.,
Sec. 3, Taipei 10657

Tel:+886-2-27080229
Fax:+886-2- 27074065
Email: team@teampm.com
http://www.teampm.com

HORIZON DESIGN—Interior (Shanghai)

Suite F, 16F, 138, Pudong Avenue,
Pudong New Area, Shanghai 200120, China

Tel:+86-21-58829179
Fax:+86-21-58829164
Email: hor@horizon-sh.com

HORIZON DESIGN—Interior (Xiamen)

1F, 106-1, Hubin 3 Li, Xiamen,
Fujian 361004, China

Tel:+86-592-5053082
FAX:+86-592-5030160
Email: lhdcl@xm-lhdcl.com